MEMORY ROYALTIES

MEMORY ROYALTIES

The Missing Link in Your Wealth Management

TODD RUSTMAN

CFA®, CFP®, CLU®, EA

Hardcover ISBN: 978-1-5445-3685-9
Paperback ISBN: 978-1-5445-3683-5
Ebook ISBN: 978-1-5445-3684-2

"The essential meaning and purpose of life is to become 'the best-version-of-yourself.'"
—Matthew Kelly, author of *The Rhythm of Life*

To everyone and everything (including Memory Royalties*!)*
that has helped shape the perspective that led to this book,
I feel blessed and grateful to be on the never-ending journey
toward the "best version of myself."

Of all the cumulative people and their teachings and learnings,
on purpose or on accident, and whether the effect came
immediately or unveiled itself over time, there is no shortage of
people or events to thank for the ever-increasing education
I continue to gain and refine.

Contents

Introduction

"Time is precious. Time is money—
time is the stuff of which life is made."
—BENJAMIN FRANKLIN

I'M A MEMBER OF GEN NEXT (NOW CALLED ALDER [www.alder.co]), a community of leaders who are committed to living a legacy that makes the country freer and better for future generations. For the past twenty years, we have gone on several annual international trips with the goal of understanding other cultures, meeting top business and government leaders, and broadening our perspectives. In 2015, we participated in a World War II review trip curated by the Stephen Ambrose historical tours (the author who wrote *Band of Brothers*, among other works). We wanted to hear from some of his interviewees firsthand and see where a few of these historical events took place. This trip was truly one of the most incredible experiences of my life.

During our time in Europe, I was overcome by the reality of war, by seeing firsthand where battles were fought and where men risked their lives for a sense of nationality and justice. It reminded me of how small our current "problems" are in the face of this overwhelming world event. We saw the bunker where Churchill had a cigar and whiskey every day and the desk that he dug his nails into so often it left deep scratches in the wood. We got to participate in interviews with people who were there, in the 1940s, when Normandy was attacked—people who parachuted, for the first time in their lives, into the heat of battle. It was sobering.

Our first evening of this trip, we ate dinner in a London restaurant, where there was a surprise guest speaker: an American World War II veteran, a very nice older gentleman in his late eighties. He spoke about his experience in the war, in the bunkers, watching friends die. Multiple times, chance and fate enabled him to escape the deaths that befell so many of his platoon members. After the war was over, he returned to the US, wondering why he was alive when so many others had died. In the following months, many soldiers who had survived (and who he knew) took their own lives, as they struggled with reintegration and survivor's guilt.

This particular veteran shared that one fateful evening, after the war, he found himself haunted by these lingering questions:

- *Why me?*

- *Why was I spared?*

- *Who else will be taken from my life?*

- *If there are no answers, why should I continue to believe my life or any life has meaning?*

He wrestled with these questions through the night and into the morning, and woke up with clarity: *I have to let these go or I'm also going to kill myself.*

At that moment, he decided what he should do next: he enrolled in a master's program, became a psychologist, and started helping veterans like himself deal with PTSD. To establish further distance from these haunting thoughts, he moved to Europe where he has lived and traveled ever since (in fact, two days after this speaking engagement, he was headed to a wedding in Greece!). Now, he shares with groups around the world. But in order to find this path forward, he had to detach himself from his experiences in the war. Like Dory in the movie *Finding Dory*, he had to "just keep swimming." He had to let go of the feelings of guilt, the questions of why, and blaze a new path.

As he began sharing with our group, this very stately-looking man started with, "I'm going to share some things with you all. I have no sense of attachment to what you do with these things, so take it or leave it. I hope you find something valuable, but if not, that's okay, too." It was a truly heartfelt and authentic invitation.

This struck an incredibly deep chord with me. Here was a distinguished, accomplished man with an incredibly self-aware and detached perspective. It wasn't that he didn't want to have an impact on us, but he was not attached to a particular outcome. He was meeting us where we were on our own journey, inviting us to find our way. And I thought, *It must be incredibly freeing to not be attached to an outcome; to share your own story so unselfishly and unprotectively.*

Our group proceeded to have an incredible trip from London, across the English Channel, to Normandy, Paris, and eventually Germany: learning, experiencing, and absorbing through all of our senses (much more impactful than the simple reading I had done back in high school and college). And, frankly (maybe even somewhat embarrassingly), I had not fully grasped the incredible life lessons made available through WWII, and how so many lives were forever changed by this catastrophic event.

Throughout the trip and other trips thereafter—and, obviously, even as I begin to write this book and share some personal thoughts and experiences—I remember him and his words. This memory has shone brightly in my life, evolving certain perspectives that I've adopted, changing how I view my sense of attachment to outcomes, and solidifying a deep belief in experiencing the world firsthand. We aren't meant to stop learning; we are perpetually becoming, and our experiences—whether good or bad—can continue to teach us priceless lessons throughout our lives. This memory, for me, continues to provide a filter through which I look at the world.

The Unhappy World of Wealth

A few years ago, I had a meeting with a new client at my Wealth Management Firm, Clarity Capital Partners. Carla had lost her husband several years prior and was still struggling a bit to find her footing after nearly fifty years of marriage. At the time, she was in her early seventies, in decent health, with two grown daughters and several grandkids across the US, and she was living in a gorgeous home in southern California.

I began our initial meeting as I typically do (especially after such a major life change), by asking Carla questions about herself:

- What were her goals, her dreams, her picture of the future?

- What did she value?

- Did she like to travel?

- Did she engage in any hobbies?

- Did she want to learn a new skill?

- If she had endless amounts of time and money wasn't an issue, what would she do?

- Where would she go?

While Carla easily named her children and grandchildren as top priorities in her life, she struggled to identify many of the answers to these questions. She felt like she was too old to learn anything new, she was afraid to travel by herself, and before we could dig too deep, she was off on a tangent about the disappointments of who the president was, the implications of rising inflation, the fear she had of losing all of their hard-earned money, the ungratefulness of her sons-in-law, and the burden of a second home her husband had insisted on purchasing in the Cayman Islands.

I wish I could say I was caught off guard by this discourse. Unfortunately, this is an exchange (or should I say monologue?!) we—as wealth managers—engage in often. Carla was an affluent individual with a lot of *life* left to live. She didn't have to worry about money. She had a family that loved her, great friends, an incredible home, and a surplus of time. But she was approaching life with what I call an "I deserve" mentality, convinced that the universe had shortchanged her and that she was a victim—of the national political climate, the stock market fluctuations, her family's entitlement, her deceased husband's decisions. Quite frankly, Carla was very unhappy and worried.

I wanted to understand *why*. Why was Carla feeling this way? What was she truly worried about? What was important to her? And how could we partner with her to develop a plan that helped her move forward, live intentionally, and experience some level of assurance and peace? This was a simple act of asking and listening—and something we do with every one of our clients—to peel back the layers of her fear and distress. What I discovered was that Carla was overwhelmed, trying to follow in her husband's footsteps of planning and executing an elaborate family trip in some exotic location. It was too much.

This is a reality that we face at our firm every single day: money does not buy happiness. In fact, *with great wealth comes great responsibility*. With great responsibility comes great stress.

I've worked in the generational wealth management world for almost three decades. During this time, I've interacted with some incredibly successful (and inspirational) people. Yet many of these people are suffering. Primarily because they live in a state of paranoia, fear, and entitlement. The wealth industry (and any training involved) is heavily focused on obtaining, growing, and protecting assets, and therefore many wealthy individuals—who have everything they could ever *need*—have lost sight of the greater meaning and joys in life.

Over time, I have come to understand that there is far more to wealth than this limited perspective. In fact, wealth opens doors to an abundance of choices and opportunities, to explore life with a sense of adventure, instead of fear and attachment bias. As with all journeys, we all have to start with that first step. In Carla's case, we began by crafting a simple plan for a domestic trip with her family—an intentional investment into meaningful memories, a.k.a. memory royalties.

A Different Way

"Since time is your most valuable asset, it's odd to spend it working with people who don't envision any long-term future together."
—PETER THEIL, author of
Bake Masters and *Zero to One*

This book is for everyone looking to regain meaning and joy. It's for those who want to live a fulfilling life, and who want to give that gift to their loved ones as well. *Memory Royalties* is for anyone who wants to do more with their money than watch it grow—it's for people who want to create memories that will last generations.

I recently had an annual check-in with Carla. She came into our office with a smile on her sun-kissed face, and immediately started telling us about the trip to Cabo she and her family just returned from. They had been celebrating her seventy-fifth birthday with an all-expenses-paid (by her!) vacation on the beach, complete with a private chef, daily excursions, and countless unrushed hours on the beach—together.

"It was a dream," she said, laughing. "I can't wait to plan the next one!"

Shocking, right? Who was this woman? What changed? Spoiler alert: we didn't press a magic happy button (wouldn't that be amazing though?). And the truth is, *we* didn't do a lot. Carla chose to journey down a path toward deeper meaning, intentionality, and freedom. She chose to turn off the news, take an inventory of her life, and start seeing things from a new perspective. We simply guided her along the way.

In *Memory Royalties*, I'm going to share some of the "secrets" Carla tapped into, some of the lessons we've learned over the years working with a variety of clients with unique stories, and perspectives that have shaped the way we view wealth and investments. My firm is great at crunching numbers and making things work. We are great at offering options and solutions for financial investments. But we are also great at coming alongside our clients to craft meaningful, joyful, and impactful stories. We like to say we are in the "life management" business.

This book is not a get-rich-quick book. In fact, you might get to the end of these pages and feel inclined to spend it all! I'm not going to tell you what to do: how to invest your money, live your life, or stick it to the man. I *am* going to offer my (and Clarity's) perspective, gleaned over years of experience working with a variety of clients who are running their own races. I stand on the shoulders of these incredible giants, and offer wisdom, insight, and encouragement. **There is more for you.**

I believe that wealth management should focus on more than growing assets. I do not believe we can cure the general sense of unhappiness and suffering that we see so often with quantitative solutions. There is no magic number in the bank that will make your life meaningful. Therefore, I am inviting you on a journey: a journey to shift how you view your wealth, invest more into meaningful memories, diversify your life, live intentionally, and ultimately run your own beautiful race.

Like the incredible speaker on my trip in Europe said, "I'm going to share some things with you all. I have no sense of attachment to what you do with these things, so take it or leave it. I hope you find something valuable, but if not, that's okay, too."

CHAPTER 1

Wealth Management Needs Fixing

"Freely ye received, freely give."
—PEPPERDINE UNIVERSITY'S MOTTO

B EFORE ATTENDING PEPPERDINE UNIVERSITY, I graduated from De Smet Jesuit High School in St. Louis, Missouri, an all-boys school that had an intense focus on spiritual growth and acts of service. I still value both of these practices today.

During my junior and senior years, I chose to work with disabled and disadvantaged youth as my service project. This was an incredibly formative experience for me to give back in this way, and it cultivated a lifelong passion in me to pursue servant leadership. I try to encompass these beliefs in everything I do.

I recently came across a book called *Awareness* by Anthony de Mello, a Jesuit priest. I was drawn to it because of my Jesuit connections and was surprised to find so many parallels to what I've discovered about attachment. (So much so that I read the entire book in one sitting!)

According to de Mello, we are often far too attached to the outcomes of our actions. For instance, we volunteer at a soup kitchen because we want to feel good about ourselves. Or we help an elderly woman put groceries in her car because we want to look like a hero. De Mello argues that if you're doing an act of service only because of the way it makes you look or how it makes you feel, you're missing the point. We should do things because we feel compelled to do them, he says. Not for an outcome.

How does this apply to wealth management, you ask? If we are only attached to the *outcome* of our earnings—e.g., accumulation and distribution—we risk missing the point of living a fulfilling life. If you don't have tangible goals for your wealth, things that truly matter to you (not for the sake of others or a perceived result), you will likely feel unhappy and unfulfilled at the end of your life.

The truth is—the view most of us have of wealth management needs improvement.

False Narratives and Arbitrary Milestones

We have limited ourselves to believe that wealth management is all about how much money we can accumulate and where we distribute said assets. But the reality is that wealth management is a balancing act that should be happening as we go.

What if we measured our output differently? What if we focused more intentionally on the long game? On creating memories and experiences that are afforded to us *because* of the assets we have accumulated? What if we shift the focus away from the accumulation itself?

You work to accumulate assets. And at the same time, you have to spend these assets in order to accrue what I call *memory royalties*. Memory royalties are tangible things you collect throughout your life—experiences, connections, moments, and knowledge that add value, meaning, and joy to your life—that you can return to over and over again. In conversations with our team, you may hear us refer to these as "memory dividends," a term coined by Bill Perkins in his book *Die with Zero*. I refer to them as memory *royalties* because every time you pull one of these memories out, it has the potential to add value again and again and again. You simply can't put a price on these!

The problem is that we've created false narratives (surrounding our assets) that color the way we manage wealth and what we're willing to invest in. I want to break down some of these misconceptions and arbitrary milestones (and poke holes in them), so we can start to look at obtaining and growing *all* assets (including memory royalties) differently.

Tech Can Do It for Me

With constantly evolving technology, we can start to believe a false narrative that wealth management is one-size-fits-all—that technology or an advisor can do it all for you. You provide the necessary information, sign some dotted lines, and poof! Magic happens.

The bottom line is it's easier to rely on others than to take an active role.

Awareness takes work. While many of our clients want to create a "set it and forget it" portfolio, we want to help people intentionally accumulate memory royalties that are specific to their lifestyle and desires. We want to help people realize their dreams. And the truth is—technology can't comprehend dreams (at least not yet!).

December 31

For many private clients and families, December 31 is a pinnacle date, *the day* that defines the financial success of the year. When you're only measuring your success by what's in the bank, this arbitrary date can hold a lot of power. But I argue that it is just that—an arbitrary date and milestone.

Ask yourself:

- If your portfolio is down on December 31, will it change your lifestyle?

- Will you do something differently on January 1 because your portfolio is down on December 31?

- Will you do something differently on January 1 if your portfolio is up on December 31?

If we're managing wealth in a more holistic way—investing in experiences, saving for long-term impact, understanding what's collectively important for you and your family—your December 31 financial status is likely a poor reflection of your long-term goals.

I had my own bout with these false narratives. I was helping a client purchase stock for his portfolio and when the clock struck midnight on December 31, he was extremely upset because the value of his new stock had dropped significantly, pushing down the total value of his portfolio on the last day of the year. However, the first of January came (as it typically does) and he realized, after some dialogue, that the short-term aberration did not change any of our planning. However, this realization required some major reframing of his long-term goals versus closing the year in a specific place.

What Does the Future Hold?

"All I want to know is where I'm going to die, so I'll never go there."
—CHARLES MUNGER

I'm going to tell you something scary (cue creepy music)… we don't know what the future holds.

I know, I know.

We like to pretend that we do! But the truth is, we have zero control of whether we'll live to be one hundred, have to care for a sick loved one, get divorced, or face a worldwide pandemic the year we retire (or decide to travel abroad).

It's human nature to plan *and* it's human nature to get set in our ways. We want to map out our wealth accumulation and exactly how, when, and where it will all go. We want a certain type of retirement. We want to die early enough, but not too early. We want to leave just the right amount of money for the next generation: enough to do *something* but not enough to do *nothing*.

Let me ask you something—has anchoring yourself to these things served you? Does attaching yourself to things you cannot control offer you happiness, peace, contentment, etc.? Because chances are, something will go wrong. And I don't mean to scare you—I mean to *invite* you into a more flexible mentality.

Typically, our attachment to things we can't control forces us into a corner. We start to think we can't learn something new. We can't try something new. We can't stray from the path. But this is a limiting way to live, and certainly a limiting way to view wealth management.

I think that our ability to adapt is our superpower! I also believe that if we *knew* our future and everything went as planned, life would most certainly be very boring.

"Deserve" versus Earn

If adaptation is our superpower, entitlement is our kryptonite.

Take a moment and fill in this blank. "I deserve _____."

Do it again. "I deserve_____."

Now, how does it make you feel? Does it make you feel happy? Excited? Fulfilled?

Or does it make you feel angry? Anxious? Short-changed?

We create shackles around ourselves when we start to repeat these phrases in our head:

- "I've paid my dues."

- "I deserve a certain amount of respect."

- "I deserve an easy retirement."

- "I deserve better WiFi on this flight, darn it!"

We create a false narrative that we are owed something and are imprisoned until we get it. This is called a *deserve mentality*, and it leads us to focus entirely on what is lacking, which keeps us trapped and clinging to our assets for dear life. To "deserve" literally breaks down to "de" and "serve"—in other words, not serving others—something that inherently violates a common value that sets us up to help other people in this lifetime.

It also breeds unhappiness. If you're constantly focused on what is owed or *should be* given to you, you can't acknowledge what you already have. "I deserve" flies directly in the face of gratitude. It prevents you from seeing the goodness, the blessings, the fullness of your life, as is. And it's ultimately an inhibitor to you experiencing a fulfilling life. How can you feel fulfilled when you think you should have more, when you are in a constant state of lack?

Furthermore, when we talk about suffering or negative situations, we use the word "me": "This happened to me and it was terrible." This perspective reflects both a *victim* mindset and a *deserve* mentality.

For instance, the stock market is down and our response might be, "This is terrible! I can't believe this is happening to me." Do you see how this strips us of power?

However, if we can look at our lives as a third-party observer and shift the perspective to "I," we can take back control and contribute to a solution or a mindset shift: "The stock market is down. I am going to stop checking it for a while because this is causing unnecessary stress."

The flipside to deserve is to *earn*. Earning is active—it's making a living. It's working hard for what you have and working hard to continue to cultivate experiences and dreams and relationships for generations to come.

I want you to earn, collect, and manage more experiences! Earning helps provide perspective and understanding, tolerance for other people, and breaks up the "us versus them" mentality. If you're busy earning (and learning!), you're busy working. And you'll find as you embrace this mentality that you won't want stuff just handed to you because—on the contrary—you've worked hard to get it.

What's the solution to this "deserve" problem?

Well, the short answer is—it's different for everyone. Great wealth management is a balancing act. Yes, my team and I want you to accumulate and protect your wealth and make wise decisions. We also want your scoreboard to reflect more than one thing. We want to manage your wealth in a way that leads to happiness, fulfillment, and contentment at the end of your days. We believe this will add tremendous value and meaning to your overall quality of life.

Self-Actualization

According to Maslow's hierarchy of needs, self-actualization is the top of the pyramid.

It's only after we find love and belonging, respect, and self-esteem that we can become our best selves. But I think if we were to focus on self-actualization first, we'd find ourselves less attached to things like status, belonging, and recognition, or in other words, *to stuff*. If we're truly on a quest to be the best versions of ourselves, we'll find that love and belonging, respect, and self-esteem are solid foundations, and we can take an active part in creating memories.

So what does it look like to continuously evaluate our wealth management plan from a self-actualizing lens? Realizing first there isn't an arrival point—a day when you'll wake up and be done with this part of the journey—how do we adjust our plans to reflect our growth as humans?

It's important for me to say that I am not immune to the ebbs and flows of the market—the low points impact me and my team, especially because these fluctuations take a toll on our clients. I struggle at times not to fall into a victim mindset, not to feel sorry for myself and for the people I work with. I have the choice in these moments to wallow in self-pity or to realize that, as part of my journey as a wealth manager, I get to learn how to embrace and learn from the ups and the downs. My account and our clients' accounts are not going to be at a high point all the time. It just doesn't work that way. I find freedom in allowing myself not to be attached to an endpoint, and this is true of the highest highs and the lowest lows—there is no final destination, and as an evolving human, I try to stay grounded in these difficult moments, to seek wisdom, to offer advice and encouragement, and to continue learning and growing. This is my journey of self-actualization.

As mentioned before, many clients want a "set it and forget it" portfolio. They want to make a choice in the moment and don't want to look at it again. The same can be true of their day-to-day lives: they want to choose an easy path that works for them and do the same things over and over again: a routine. They have one destination in mind—accumulation—and they push forward with laser focus on this one thing. But the problem with this mentality is that it doesn't account for changes along the way, for diversification or for fun, joy, and deeper meaning.

Instead, I want to encourage you to take the "destination" out of the equation. There is no set point in our lives when we "arrive," when we have nothing more to do, experience, or become. We can continue diversifying our experiences to reflect this ongoing journey, as our interests shift, as we get older, as our families grow. This means we look at our lives as a whole and intentionally create memories: with our families, with our colleagues, and with ourselves.

The truth is that you're not going to get more time.

> *"It is later than you think."*
> —SENECA

And, typically, while our wealth increases, our time *decreases*. Simply put: the older we get, the less time we have. Therefore, our time becomes more valuable as we get older.

This means two things:

1. You should be paid more to give up what's remaining of your time doing the things that bring value to your life; and

2. You should aim to spend all of the time you have left well (again, not that we know what that amount is!).

Our job, as wealth managers at our firm, is not simply to manage your wealth but to help ensure that you are investing your money into experiences that are meaningful to you—big and small—and push you closer to self-actualization. Whether it's a weekly night out with your grandchild or an all-expenses-paid vacation for ten of your closest friends, we can help crunch the numbers and make a plan so that these experiences, and a life of impact, are a part of your wealth management plan.

When it comes to wealth management, you can't "set it and forget it." *You* are changing, so your journey toward self-actualization is changing. This means you need to evaluate and *re*evaluate your goals, financially and personally. What you want to spend your money experiencing today will likely be different tomorrow.

A Life of Impact

During the heart of COVID-19, when Brad Pitt was accepting a Golden Globe Award for Best Supporting Actor in *Once Upon a Time in Hollywood*, he said, "Hey! If you see a chance to be kind to someone tomorrow, take it. I think we need it." It made me think about the imprint I'm leaving behind and the true legacy I want to leave my children and grandchildren. This has nothing to do with my assets, but I can spend my money in a way that reflects this desire and supports this impact.

So many of us live to work. Our job titles and wealth accumulation become destinations that we think can define our success and value as humans. That's why we get tangled up in false narratives and arbitrary milestones—we get so caught up in this rat race that we don't recognize these are simply mile markers. The promotion, the number on your bank statement, the second house you purchased—these are not the things that give your life true meaning.

Impact is different for every person, but it starts with defining it for yourself. What kind of impact do you want to have? Not financially—but spiritually, emotionally, and physically. Defining this (and redefining it over and over again) will influence how you distribute your assets and view your money.

I want to be a peaceful warrior. This is the impact I want to have on my family, my employees, and our clients. I want to be a person that listens well, that shows empathy and compassion, but that fights to the death for the people I care about. I truly believe that every person I interact with has something to offer, and I want to continue to be open to receive the wisdom and insight each person brings to the table. I'm not perfect, but I work on embodying a peaceful warrior daily, because having this vision in mind for my life helps me engage in my work, my conversations, and my experiences differently. It changes my perspective and allows me to look for growth opportunities.

You Can Do and Be Anything You Want

"Sometimes you win, sometimes you ~~lose~~ learn."
—JOHN C. MAXWELL

Remember playing on the playground when you were a child? In one moment, you were a pizza chef, spinning imaginary pizzas in the air and dishing them up to your friends. The next moment, you were a frantic doctor, trying to save your friend from an imaginary broken leg that would most surely be the death of him. You could do or *be* anything you wanted!

As we get older, we start to believe "you can't do this" and "you can't do that." Oh, and there's also: "You really *shouldn't* do that." We lose our childlike wonder of the world and things become drudgery. We get set on a path and we stop thinking of new ideas; we stop our willingness to change and adapt. When we choose this path, we become more fragile, small hiccups feel like earthquakes, and we're unable to pivot and adapt because we are so set in our ways.

Is this really how we want to live?

The majority of the world is trying to chart a path for you and tell you how to feel. But it's important to keep a childlike perspective that you can do and be anything you want. That kid on the playground, wearing a cape, on a mission to teleport and save the world—that kid still exists inside of you. What would it look like to tap into that excitement, that spontaneity, that expectation that life has so much more for you?

I desire for you to rediscover childlike wonder in your life, to realize that *because* of your assets, you have the ability to explore the world, to make deeper connections, and to run your *own* race. You don't have to do the same things every day, you don't have to go on the same predictable vacation, you don't have to trod the *same* well-worn path. I want to help open your eyes to all of the possibilities.

When you are an active participant in crafting your wealth management strategy, your strategy becomes fluid and changes *with* you, as you discover all you can do and be. Our job, as a wealth management advisor, is to help expose the journey and act as a resource, so you only make *new* mistakes—you only pay tuition *once* as we catalog what worked and what didn't work along the way. My team and I want to guide you on an inward exploration of what it means to be whoever you are and pursue experiences and outlets that express that.

My early Jesuit beginnings in high school have influenced everything I do. The firm I founded (Clarity Capital Partners) is rooted in principles I learned there: genuine connection, outrageous generosity, and service with thoughtfulness and care.

You have the opportunity to do something incredible with your life! And the way you manage your wealth should reflect your ultimate purpose, whatever that is for you. Defining this at the forefront of your wealth management journey gives you the opportunity to reverse engineer for your purpose and evaluate whether this purpose and plan have the potential for long-term impact.

But first, we have to shift our perspective. If we're too consumed with fear and bogged down by negativity, we can't embrace the possibilities. We can't even see all of them! So let's take a moment to acknowledge our addiction to bad news and start to shift our gaze toward the good.

CHAPTER 2

The Future is Bright

*"We share about 97 percent of the crucial building blocks
of life—carbon, hydrogen, nitrogen, carbon, phosphorus,
and sulfur—with the rest of the galaxy."*
—JAMIE WHEAL, *Recapture the Rapture*

IN THE MOVIE *TRADING PLACES*, TWO MILLIONAIRE
brokers (the Duke brothers) make a $1 bet to see if they
can turn a hustler (Billy Ray Valentine) into a successful businessman and a successful businessman (Louis Winthorpe)
into a hustler—the brokers wanted to see which was stronger,
nature or nurture. They frame Winthorpe for a crime he
didn't commit, fire him from the brokerage firm, and replace
him with Valentine.

When Valentine and Winthorpe find out about the scheme, they turn the tables on the brokers. They make their own bet, and overnight, the Dukes lose everything. Valentine concludes, "You know, it occurs to me that the best way to hurt rich people is by turning them into poor people."

I think he was really getting at something.

However, I'd take this one step further and say the best way to hit rich people where it hurts is to make them *afraid* to turn into poor people. The fear of becoming poor is very real to many people, so their response can be to protect their money like Ebenezer Scrooge. If this is the case, the goal then becomes to shield their nest egg from all creditors, invaders, taxes, inflation, family members, etc. They then spend their lives trying to avoid this potential pain at all costs, and this can result in missing out on truly living. They can become *paralyzed* by fear. And much of this fear is fueled by false, negative information the media feeds us.

Addicted to Bad News

In 1997, Geri Weis-Corbley, a former Washington, DC, television and news producer, launched the Good News Network to help spread *positive* news stories. It features stories from big news outlets, like CNN and NBC, but it also curates original content from independent authors and columnists. The one thing all these different contributors have in common? The stories and articles have to be *positive*.

The Good News Network is still around today, and even though the outlet reports on current news, its viewership pales in comparison to Fox, CNN, or CBS. Not surprisingly, viewer numbers rise when times are especially tough. On the regular, however, we simply don't go looking for good news. We are far too hooked on negativity, and sadly, we don't even realize it because there are countless ways to consume bad information through various social media platforms, talk show hosts, regular news channels, emails, etc.

Media will use any tactic it can to keep you engaged, and often this entails heightened, exaggerated language that gets you worked up, upset, and angry. Language like that implies an urgency and an impending doom about all matters, all the while with one goal in mind—to keep you sitting there, glued to your news source, petrified. "Stay tuned. After the commercials, we're going to tell you more..."

And here's what it does: it changes your view of reality. It makes you scared. Knowing that fear is one of the most powerful motivators in human behavior, all of this bad news leads you to stay frozen in place. You postpone your trip to Mexico because of danger on the border. You cancel your Disney trip with your grandkids because of an active shooter in Virginia. You hold off on that investment because the market is volatile (when is the market *not* volatile?), the economy is going to crash, and this man or woman might get elected president.

This negativity then spills over into how we view and manage our wealth and our time. Media is mainly fixated on negative volatility, spinning doomsday stories about our investments, extrapolating to an unrealistic endpoint, making the particular threat seem more real than it is, and ultimately further stoking the fire of fear. Even when the media alludes to success or growth, it often goes hand-in-hand with a good dose of skepticism and suggestions that this type of positivity might be "too good to be true." But, hey—stay tuned and find out why!

Upside versus Downside Volatility

We often talk negatively about the market being volatile. But volatility describes both downward and upward movement. We actually want and *need* volatility. However, volatility is not necessarily welcome when it's down, and we work hard to limit downside volatility (called semi-variance). When the market is down, it challenges our belief that we did the right thing. Therefore, we look for asymmetric returns to the upside because we want *upside* volatility. But the truth is: we can't have the upside without the downside. There's no way around this.

If you have a truly diversified portfolio, there will always be something you don't like. If you can look at your portfolio of stocks and investments and everything is performing exactly the same, you're not diversified. And we need diversification, with position sizing, so that in instances where some of our investments go down for a period of time, we still have areas of our portfolio that hold or even increase their value during that time.

Anthony de Mello says, "You keep insisting, I feel good because the world is right! Wrong! The world is right because I feel good. That's what all the mystics are saying."

We often focus on external factors to determine our internal peace. Many of our clients only feel settled and satisfied when the market is up—this is when the world feels right to them. But this is the wrong connection. If we are running our own race, creating memory royalties, and being intentional about living with a purpose, our sense of "all's right with the world" will not be dependent on a volatile market (that swings both up and down!).

This mentality plays out in our memory royalties, as well. We tend to think that we "deserve" only positive experiences all of the time. So when we have to wait too long for a waiter to take our order, when our flight is delayed, when our angsty teenager won't plaster a smile on his face on our tropical vacation, we immediately go into an anxious, angry, or disappointed state. If we want to access this sense of inner peace, we have to learn to ride the waves. We have to find a sense of inner peace that isn't dependent on an outcome.

Not all of your memory royalties will be positive. You'll go on a trip that falls flat. You'll read a book you don't like. You'll try a hobby that you just aren't very good at! In the same way you experience volatility in the market, you can and will experience volatility in your life. Experiencing the good and the bad, the ups and the downs, is a necessary part of truly living. I want to suggest that the downward volatility in your experiences helps you appreciate when things are truly up. And I also sincerely believe that you can find something good, even in the worst of situations.

See the Good

Because of the constant influx of bad news, sometimes we have to *work* to see the good and put all of this negativity into perspective. The truth is, we have so much more than we will ever need, and instead of buying into the impending doom stories, we can choose to see the good.

How, you ask?

First of all, turn off the TV! Put your phone down. Go look outside. Go on a walk. Learn a new skill. Have a conversation with a loved one. As you participate in new activities, learn new things, and choose a different way, you create new neural pathways in your brain. These neural pathways are what keep you truly living—they help you experience real emotions, have meaningful interactions, and create lasting memories. Choosing to do something different can help you look outside of the negativity, to see the good that exists just outside your own front door.

Another way to train yourself to see the good is to recognize that things could be worse. This isn't so much a game of comparison, but a shift in perspective. If you have a difficult time recognizing what is good in your own life, if you're wallowing in self-pity or fear, perhaps take a moment to consider how it could be worse. Then, allow this to change your focus from what is not right to what is good in your life.

Right now, it's sixty degrees in Newport Beach. I'm watching the sun come up, and it's going to be a beautiful day. Even though there is political unrest in our country and abroad, a global pandemic underway, and many unknowns with my teenage kids—none of it has to affect my perspective *today* or my investment in my *future*. It doesn't have to impact my goals or family. Not that I turn a blind eye to everything, but I *do* choose to let it hold an *appropriate* amount of power over my outlook and my personal decisions.

When we choose to see the good, and focus on *it* and not fear, we don't wallow for weeks in misery or frantically react to situations. We spend our time *living*. Again, we don't suddenly arrive at a destination and declare that we have lived. This is an ongoing process. Every day, we choose to embrace life and the new experiences that come our way. We make a commitment to work on ourselves, to engage with others, and to see the good all around us.

Abundance and Gratitude

As we shift our gaze toward the good that exists, it opens us up to observe abundance. We live in an era of possibility. Technology makes so much available to us—communication, travel, business opportunities, wealth management. Heck, I can even get my groceries delivered to my front door! However, instead of recognizing this as abundance, instead of thinking, *We are the luckiest*, our response is often entitlement. We think because of increased accessibility, everything should be easy and everything should work all of the time. We think we "deserve" all of this abundance, and therefore when things don't quite go our way, we get angry, frustrated, and lash out. Or we choose to live with a scarcity mentality, constantly afraid of not having enough, hoarding our assets, assuming the worst, and feeding the spirit of negativity. Or perhaps we see ourselves as victims, focusing on what's lacking, thinking we should have more, afraid the world is out to get us.

Because you're reading this book, I can assume that you either have funds to purchase it, access to a public library, or a friend who lent it to you. This alone points to a level of abundance. The fact that you have time to read a book implies that you aren't spending every waking hour simply trying to survive or to make ends meet. What a wonderful thing—you are able to spend some of your time investing in yourself, growing as a human, and becoming better. This ability to devote to yourself is an incredible privilege, something worth taking the time to be thankful for.

The antidote to this victim mentality and this spirit of entitlement is gratitude. While it may be a simple word that gets thrown around a lot these days, it's not quite as easy to master. It requires intentional practice to cultivate a spirit of gratitude. But as we integrate thankfulness into our everyday lives, it does become easier and it honestly changes everything. It shifts how we see our own individual world and it also helps us take the reins and realize that we are the author of our own fate. We have an abundance of choices. And that alone is something to be grateful for.

There is endless research that shows the positive effects of gratitude. It creates a sense of peace, harmony, happiness, and joy, even when things in your life don't look the way you want them to. Gratitude allows you to fully enjoy your experiences, to connect with others more deeply, and to foster better resiliency when facing difficult situations. Gratitude makes your life richer. It also opens you up to see how rich your life already is.

In the past, I've implemented a few different gratitude practices (I like to change it up when certain exercises start to feel stale or repetitive). For a long time, I kept a gratitude journal, where I would write down three things I was thankful for before I went to sleep at night. This has extra benefits because a lot of healing (both physical and emotional) occurs when we're asleep, and putting positive thoughts into our head before we go to bed and start dreaming helps strengthen and expedite this mental healing process. I also engage in a lot of internal dialogue, particularly when I find myself falling into a victim mindset. I think about how the situation could be worse, or I vent all of the negative stuff until I start uncovering the positive spin. Most of our negative situations are learning experiences in disguise—we just have to be willing to discover the underlying lessons and learn from them.

And again, this is a process. I fall prey to negativity and the deserve mentality just like anyone else. We all get off track, and it's okay—these are opportunities to reset, get back on track, grow, and become more self-aware.

If you're choosing gratitude, it becomes more difficult to give in to the voices of negativity that surround you. If you're taking the time to recognize abundance, it's harder to buy into the lies that you don't have enough, that you're going to lose it all, or that someone or something is out to get you. If you are shifting the focus from what you don't have to what you do have and intentionally fostering a spirit of thankfulness, you are continuously opening yourself up to more goodness.

Your Inner Tribe

One of the most amazing choices we have in life is who we surround ourselves with, our chosen families or our inner tribes. These are the people that you get to do life with, through shared experiences, purposeful conversations, and years of relationships. Therefore, it's important to choose these people with care, to fill your inner tribe with people that bring insight, accountability, and goodness into your world. When you're surrounded by positive, inspiring people, it opens up your world.

A lot of my inner tribe has been obsessed with Cabo for many years, and they kept telling me that I needed to go, that I would love it. I grew up going to Cancun with my family, back when there was only one hotel and one restaurant and Playa del Carmen wasn't a thing yet. My inner tribe knew all of the fond memories I had from those times with my family, but Cancun is crazy now, and it's hard to get to. They told me—"Cabo is only a two-hour flight and the prices are right and you can fully disconnect there." When I finally went, I realized that they were absolutely right. And of course they were! They know my likes and dislikes; they know what I value in a vacation destination; they know *me*. This is what an inner tribe is for, to encourage you to try new things, to point you in the right direction, and to share their knowledge and experiences to make your life more fulfilling.

One of the most valuable parts of friendship is the feedback loop, having a trusted person observe your choices and experiences, someone who can offer advice and insight, someone to warn you when you're going to make a foolish mistake or pay tuition a second time! You learn from each other, and therefore your experiences have a splatter effect. Life is far brighter when you get to share it with other people.

Invest in a Better Life

You have the choice to invest in a better life, but this requires a shift in the narrative about wealth management. While our firm has tons of investments that we could show you, many times the best investment is into yourself. Learning a new skill, pursuing a new accreditation, traveling with your loved ones, making new memories—all of these things can combat the negativity, fear, and entitlement that steal so much joy and meaning from your life.

Learning is "earning" with an "L": for every new opportunity or concept or even mistake that we encounter, we *earn* memory royalties. We earn lessons, experiences, skills, and ideas. I don't want to stop learning (and earning). I truly believe that learning a new skill or furthering my education is one of the most valuable investments I could make. I come from a long line of teachers—learning, curiosity, and knowledge were highly valued in my family. In fact, I'm in a business where I can't stop learning! Our clients are constantly teaching me new things (and a lot of the time, they don't even know it!). Their life experiences, wisdom, and perspective help shape how I do business, how I raise my family, and what I offer to other clients. I absolutely love this part of my job and am truly blessed.

I also believe that the world is a classroom, and therefore I invest a ton into travel. Even when these experiences go awry, they pay back a hundredfold. Seeing other countries, meeting different people, and experiencing new cultures—all of this helps put our own lives in perspective, creates memory royalties, and fosters a sense of hopefulness and meaning.

The Gift of Influence

"Life grows relative to one's investment in it."
—MARC BENIOFF, CARLYE ADLER, *Behind the Cloud*

Because of the advent of time, the future is so bright. Not only do we have access to more and a longer life span, we also have the ability to share our life experiences across three or four generations. We have the gift of influence by involving others in our memory royalties, that they might repeat and share these experiences with the next generation.

Many war heroes won't share their experiences with their wife or kids upon returning home. They want to protect their family from the horrors they faced, to shield them from the hopelessness and negativity. They need time and space away from the trauma to process and understand their experiences. But—they *do* tend to share their wartime experiences with their grandchildren, when they start to feel their mortality clock ticking. By this time, they feel enough distance to glean understanding from what they saw and experienced. They feel far enough away from the horrors to impart wisdom and lessons to those next in line.

This is true across the board. As you get older, you start to think about your mortality. You want to pass on what you've learned and share your passions, hopes, and dreams with the next generation. And with longer life spans, we have so much more opportunity to make mistakes, to experience successes, and to pass all of these things down through generations. We get to expedite wisdom, to shortcut the journey as we stand on the shoulders of giants. Because we can catalog our experiences—orally and written—we can learn from those that went before us and excel much quicker. We can also make better choices: by observing the failures and mistakes of others, we can choose to be better people and make a more positive impact on the world.

Shifting our view of wealth management begins with recognizing the negative baggage and perspectives we've bought (or continue to buy) into. While the media wants to keep us engaged with bad news and negative outlooks, we have a choice: to let this affect our daily lives or to step away from this constant reel and realize our future is bright. We have more than enough, so much to be grateful for, and the means to invest differently.

You can choose to live like Ebenezer Scrooge or Mr. Burns, and hoard your money until the day you die, or you can use it to curate new experiences, share your life with those you love, and create long-lasting memories that will make the future even brighter. Now more than ever, you have the potential to be so much more complete and fulfilled. You have so many more choices. The future is truly unwritten, and through intentional investment and access to knowledge and experiences, you can pour *more* of yourself into your future and legacy. The heart of our firm is to invest in the whole person. To help our clients live happier, more fulfilling lives. And most of the time, this has nothing to do with accumulation. It has everything to do with investing money into diverse outlets, like memory royalties, your inner tribe, or a new skill set, which leads to a very bright future.

CHAPTER 3

Focus on Memory Royalties

"Vagabonding is about gaining the courage to loosen your grip on the so-called certainties of this world. Vagabonding is about refusing to exile travel to some other, seemingly more appropriate, time of your life. Vagabonding is about taking control of your circumstances instead of passively waiting for them to decide your fate."
—ROLF POTTS, *Vagabonding*

One Thing(s)

Curly: You know what the secret of life is?

Mitch: No, what?

Curly: (holds up his leather-gloved hand and points his index finger) This.

Mitch: Your finger?

Curly: One thing, just one thing.

Mitch: That's great, but what's the one thing?

Curly: That's what you've got to figure out.

In this famous exchange from the movie *City Slickers*, Curly suggests that the secret of life is to find your "one thing." And while I actually think your one thing can change, that you can have multiple "one things" throughout your life, I think he points to something very important in crafting a life that holds true value and enjoyment, and this is the idea of running your own race.

This doesn't mean we become unmalleable, fixed on one thing for our entire lives. But it does mean we live with intentionality, giving thought to how our decisions—vacations, investment allocations, time blocking—align with our overall intention, the legacy we want to leave behind, the impact that we want to have, and what we want to be remembered for. It also means we look forward, toward the future, and let go of the past that we cannot change.

We are—every single one of us—very different and unique. We bring to the table various gifts, talents, passions, joys, and hopes. You name it. And all of these intricacies inform our decisions, relationships, and one-of-a-kind journeys. But we have to listen, reflect, and allow these things to color what we do and ultimately *who* we are. We have to *know* and *own* who we are, in order for our life to flourish.

Running your own race is an ever-evolving learning process. Your own successes are something to be built upon or contrasted against. Your failures are something to be reflected upon and learned from. These experiences can launch you in new directions and introduce you to new ideas, people, or perspectives.

Memory Royalties

Many years ago, a client of mine arrived at our annual check-in with a lot of questions. He was a self-made businessman, had done quite well for himself, and was still enjoying working hard in his "later years." He had recently read *Die with Zero* and it made him wonder—*what is this all about? Does it really serve me and the world to accumulate this pot of money and do nothing of value with it?*

And it struck me then that this is a difficult but necessary part of our job—to help our clients discover meaningful ways to invest their money. Not just crunching numbers and ensuring there will be a surplus at the end, but truly digging into this idea of meaning—how will you spend your money to create a meaningful life? How will you invest in experiences and people in a way that makes you feel fulfilled at the end of your days? I call these *memory royalties*.

Memory royalty, *noun:* A memory royalty is an **asset** that **doesn't tarnish** with age. It can be shared with loved ones or enjoyed solo. **It's an investment, not an expense,** that you can access at a moment's notice. It adds variety to your life and possibly helps slow down time. **It does not turn into a liability as we get older, like so many other tangible assets.** A shared memory royalty can also deepen connections with others, so life is celebrated and enjoyed.

Each person is different. Every one of us arrives at the table with baggage, expectations, hopes, and fears that drive our individual stance on wealth, investments, and spending. If you inherited your money, you might feel guilty about it. You might not want to work as hard as your parents because they weren't around and their work ruled their lives. Maybe you've sacrificed for every cent you own and therefore are more protective of your money. Perhaps you came from nothing and you don't want to return to a place of less or "lack." As you map out a financial plan, your history matters, your attachment to your money matters, and the impact you want to have matters.

But often our clients (and us wealth managers) place the focus on money alone. While I can make a lot of numbers work for a client, I can't define what will make them feel fulfilled. That's why I think it's vital to interlace investment conversations with the question, "What would make your life feel more fulfilling? What more do you want to do while you're in this world?"

One of the most important things in life is our journey to wholeness, uncovering who we are, and living a life that is fulfilling. If we were to spend our entire life in one room, reading books all day long, we wouldn't be out experiencing life. We *need* real-life experiences and relationships to fully realize our potential and what we have to offer the world. While not everyone can be Alexander the Great or Kobe Bryant, and while most of us won't have a book written about our lives, we each have great potential to impact the people around us, to invest time into our tribe, and to leave an invaluable imprint on the "world" that truly knew us!

Running Your Own Race

It's easy today—with the prevalence of social media and quick access to information—to let others define success or purpose for you. In order to establish your definition of fulfillment, you have to stop looking at other people to determine who you are.

You have to run your own race.

What does running your own race have to do with memory royalties? Everything! Memory royalties add to your uniqueness and are a tangible demonstration of what is valuable and meaningful to you.

When you hone in on your unique goals and desires, it becomes easier to say **hell no** to the things that don't matter to you and **hell yes** to opportunities that are going to increase your sense of fulfillment. You can then identify memory royalties that add value to your life, and quit obsessing over what other people are doing or what's "right and wrong."

- Do you want to pay for your children's education? Or ensure they contribute to the world and (hopefully!) have more happiness in their life than sadness?

- Do you want to buy your son or daughter a house? Help him or her start a biz?

- Do you want to spend a month in Italy? With whom? Solo, spouse, family, or friends?

Once you have the answers, go deeper:

- Do these things align with the race you're running?

- Are they going to offer you meaning, fulfillment, and pleasure?

Running your own race can also become a shield against comparison, bitterness, and the "I deserve" attitude we talked about in Chapter 1. When you invest time and money into things that truly matter, you can stop worrying about what your neighbor is doing, what you're still owed, and what's lacking in your life. When you intentionally invest into experiences and people that matter to you, you feel more fulfilled, find more gratitude, and can set aside feelings of entitlement and disappointment.

Running Someone Else's Race

In this social media–saturated world, the temptation to idolize celebrities and compare ourselves to others stands in direct opposition to the idea of running our own race. While we may get a glimpse into these people's lives, we don't actually *know* their memory royalties. We don't know how they feel about their unique path, and we can't actually become them—there's only one Kobe. Oftentimes, we only really glimpse a fraction of someone else's journey and don't get to see the hardship, the sacrifices, and the struggle that got them to where they are. Our obsession with celebrities and top athletes can be truly futile, yet—when properly framed—serve as an inspiration to point to what is possible.

You are far better off spending time in your own feedback loop and actively processing how you can add to your own memory royalties. And while you're at it, you can be thankful for your own precious time that isn't hijacked by autographs, grocery store fan selfies, or back-to-back gigs that someone else scheduled for you! (Celebrity status isn't all it's cracked up to be.)

Maybe it's not becoming famous that appeals to you. Maybe it's a number in the bank, an imaginary accumulation or destination that causes you to feel like what you currently have is lacking. Maybe you compare yourself to others who have more (or appear to have more…). Any one of these obsessions is robbing you of charting your own path and finding a sense of gratitude in all that you *do* have. Focusing on your own race helps keep attachments at more of a minimum, as you resist the urge to compare yourself to others or covet what others have or have done.

Not every venture will be awesome or incredible—and that's okay! Since you are running your own race, no one is judging you for this, and it's all part of the process. Much like dating helps us determine who we *don't* want to be tied to for life (as much as it helps us find the right person), these less-than-perfect experiences help us go, "Nope, don't want to do that again!" They offer us insight and lessons to be implemented in the future.

For me, running my race includes investing in our clients. We get to be an observer, to glean wisdom and insight from our clients' successes, experiences, and "failures" (we like to call these "tuition" or "learning experiences"). We gain perspective about different cultures, personalities, and beliefs. We don't spend time comparing ourselves to our clients because each one has their own race to run. But their race can inform and affect mine and help me define and redefine what matters to me and what direction I want to go in.

For example, I love to travel. And my family loves to travel, so we invest money and time into these types of memory royalties. But for many of our clients who have spent years traveling for work, their goal is to *stop* traveling when they are retired. This makes sense, right? But should my love of traveling influence their decision to settle down in retirement? Or should their desire to settle down make me second guess my trip overseas? Absolutely not.

Running your own race means exactly that—doing what's best for you, regardless of what's best for someone else.

ENGAGE YOUR SENSES

When you enjoy a glass of wine (my favorite is a glass of Cabernet from Levendi Winery! Sorry, not sorry for the promo!), taste isn't the most important sense you engage—it's smell. That's why we swirl the wine in the glass, to get the full aroma. Your sense of smell will ultimately determine what you like about a particular wine. Now, imagine if you only read about wine in a book. "It tastes like tobacco, raspberries, and earth." You'd probably think, *What a crock.* But if you were to actually smell and taste this wine—you'll get it! It does actually taste like this crazy combination of things. And while reading about it won't give you the full experience, it will help you understand the vocabulary and perhaps enjoy the experience that much more.

The same is true of our memory royalties. It's not enough to just read about experiences and to be aware of opportunities. To get the full meaning, we have to actually leave the comfort of our routine lives sometimes—to taste, see, and feel something. To eat a street taco in Mexico. To strum the strings of a guitar. To feel your heart pound when you make a risky investment. To laugh with your children on a roller coaster. These are the things that will actually add value and meaning to your life.

It's also important to note that not every experience is going to be perfect—so try not to be attached to a certain outcome. If all of your experiences are easy, fun, and light-hearted, you can't fully appreciate them. Opposites allow us to feel the impact of an experience and distinguish the differences. One of my favorite clients and best friends recently took his daughter to Puerto Rico. It was right after the holidays, in the middle of a COVID-19 surge, and many places were closed. While he enjoyed spending time with his daughter, he didn't have the best experience in Puerto Rico. But he's already talking about his next trip, his next memory royalty (but not to Puerto Rico). Despite your planning and your best intentions, you will have disappointing experiences. But hopefully more often than not, you'll have incredible experiences that help your life feel full, well-rounded, and joyful.

INVESTING INTO YOUR INNER TRIBE

Your time is your most precious resource. And we spend a lot of our time with other people. Sometimes people offer incredible values (even if we don't agree with them!) and sometimes people can suck the life out of us. So when we think about memory royalties and this idea of investing in things that matter to us, it's important to consider the relationships we want to pour our limited time into.

When you think about the people in your inner circle, your tribe, if you will, take some time to evaluate if these people are bringing value to your life, and if you're offering value to them. What lessons do you learn from them? How are you helping them grow? It's important to not only pursue meaningful relationships, but also to share experiences with these people. Experiences with others are incredible memory royalties, opportunities to add meaning and value to life.

Memory royalties also include engaging conversations that help enlighten, inspire, and connect you with your peers. That's why it's so important to participate in deeper conversations with your close friends, so you can understand new perspectives, ask questions, and share your thoughts, dreams, and goals. Technology has made it increasingly easier to connect and share with other people, offering us so many avenues to touch the lives of the people around us, and we should be using these tools to do just that—to connect in truly meaningful and honest ways.

While it's important to have people in your inner tribe that are equally yoked, it's also important *not* to get all of your advice and viewpoints from a "mirror." If you are only spending time with people who look and think exactly like you, you're not getting a well-rounded opinion or engaging opportunities to be challenged and grow. Considering different perspectives and counterpoints is crucial as you determine who you are and what is important to you. Instead of looking for a "mirror," we can think about relationships as looking through a new "window" or opening a "door" to new insights and perspectives.

BLESSEDLY GIVE

I believe most people want to make the world a better place, if given the opportunity. If you only have one goal in mind and that goal is to accumulate, then you won't think about the gifts you have to share or the impact you want to have. And I'm not simply referring to giving away money (though if it floats your boat, go for it).

In order to give, we first have to take the time to recognize what we have. Maybe that's time. Maybe it's a skill. Maybe it's knowledge or wisdom or guidance. Maybe it's a mistake that you've made (a.k.a. lesson that you've learned!) that you want to share with others so that they don't have to make that same error. Once we recognize our gifts, we have to stop and smell the roses. Look around. Who is in need of what you have to offer? How can you give your gifts away?

I am an acts of service guy (in other words, I probably won't be sending you flowers or writing you affirming notes). How does this translate into blessedly giving? When I meet with clients, I internalize their struggles. I don't like the idea of giving advice; I don't believe in telling people what they *should* do, and I think most people can solve their own problems if given the time and space. But I do believe in providing options, and I like to pull from my experiences—both personally and vicariously through many friends and clients—to help people on their journey, to meet them where they are, and to be helpful without criticism or judgment. I am a sounding board, and I like to think that I help people only make *new* mistakes.

People often think of "giving"—particularly when an individual has a lot of wealth—in terms of money or time. But the truth is, our memory royalties become gifts we can give away. The stories, the lessons, the mistakes, the knowledge, the beauty, the sadness—all of these experiences are incredible treasures that we get to share with people. And the amazing thing is that the "giving away" blesses us too. When we share these memories, we get to remember their impact, importance, and lessons all over again.

COMPOUNDING MEMORIES

Albert Einstein once said, "Compound interest is the eighth wonder of the world. He who understands it, earns it; he who doesn't, pays it." Compound interest is a powerful force. You invest small increments each day or each year, and suddenly— thirty years down the road—you are absolutely shocked by how much this small investment has increased over time.

The same is true of memory royalties. You invest in regular breakfast dates with a friend or annual trips with loved ones or volunteering at a local school. Small investments of time that build over the days and years—the lessons you learn, the people you meet, the bonds you forge, and the memories you make. You share these experiences with others, either physically or through conversation, creating further memories. Your investment grows exponentially as it impacts those you share it with: inspiring others, changing lives, and making the world just a little bit better.

ONGOING LEARNING

One of your greatest superpowers, in a world where we live longer and where things don't go our way all the time, is your ability to learn new things, invest in yourself, and acquire new skills.

If one of our clients says, "I want to learn how to sing," we think, "Yes!" These types of memory royalties are incredibly worthwhile endeavors to broaden horizons. We would much rather see you invest in yourself and experience other facets of life than invest in things that you have less control over, like cryptocurrency or high-risk securities. As we invest our clients' capital in the traditional financial sense, we don't (nor do our clients) have absolute control over outcomes—that's why we recommend diversification, position sizing, and "reverse engineering" for capital disbursements. On the other hand, investing in an experience, a vacation, or a new skill will undoubtedly yield results.

I have an internal compass that wants to uncover new rocks because I sincerely believe that you can get ideas from anywhere! Remember Peter Lynch? He's one of the most successful investors of all time. He would go to the mall with his children and wife, observe where they spent money, and discover retail trends that would help inform his investments. We're talking about the shopping mall! Now, this was long before the internet, but you get where I'm coming from. Ideas are everywhere! We can learn from anything and anyone. We just have to be open to observe and receive them.

My interest in learning even extends to distributed ledger technology (DLT), and I received a certificate in blockchain and cryptocurrency through the Digital Assets Council of Financial Professionals (DACFP). Who knows where that will lead?! This posture not only keeps me young but also encourages a sense of wonder and curiosity that helps make my daily life meaningful. This is something my team also strives for because we coach our clients to do the same.

If your whole focus is work and accumulation, what happens when these things are taken away? Many of our clients think they can get their company or their portfolio to a certain point where they can breathe a sigh of relief. But I haven't seen this actually happen. There's almost always more to do. The "destinations" they so desperately strive for aren't real. In fact, there isn't an ultimate destination in life because there's more to know and more to experience—there are more memory royalties you can invest in and capture. That's why I see so much value in the pursuit of knowledge and connection. "With all thy getting, get understanding."

Who are you? How much of life is left? What does that life look like? Skills, hobbies, and experiences will help define meaning and life outside of monetary accumulation and hopefully give you a greater sense of wellbeing, impact, and fullness.

And when you think about it, every physical asset becomes a liability. This is something important to keep in mind as you consider purchasing physical assets—second or third homes, airplanes, boats, etc. Every one of these adds an element of stress and commitment to your life. Not only do you have the cost of keeping it up, you also inherit the guilt of not using it enough *or* the sacrifice of time *to* use it. I like to think of these assets like Marie Kondo talks about your closet—if it doesn't bring you joy or add value to your life, get rid of it. Apply this same concept to tangible assets and invest into memories instead.

MORE THAN MONEY

"You are a thinking person, 'I think. Therefore I am,' but in reality, the thoughts you are thinking are most likely working against you. The highest percentage of the time, almost all the time, your thoughts are looping through your subconscious thought patterns."

—MELISSA FEICK,
A Radical Approach to the Akashic Records

Melissa Feick, a vibrational ascension leader, references research on the brain in her book, *A Radical Approach to the Akashic Records*. Daily, there are 50,000 to 70,000 thoughts running around in your head. Researchers say that this number is a conservative estimate.

No wonder you're exhausted!

But if that surprises you, it may blow your mind to know that 90–98 percent of these thoughts are the same ones you had yesterday! That's right—your mind is in a constant loop, thinking and rethinking the same things over and over again. We are creatures of habit, and this attachment to predictability often carries into every aspect of our lives: the way we drive to work, what we eat for breakfast, our evening routine, and certainly how and where we spend our money.

Life is about so much more than money.

When I first got into the finance business, one of the stories they would tell us was, "You've never met anyone on their deathbed saying they wish they had saved less."

This makes me laugh now. Have you actually ever *met* anyone on their deathbed who talks about their savings? Save less, save more—who cares? You're dying. And you can't take your money with you.

The client that was impacted so profoundly by *Die with Zero* has shifted his mentality about how he invests his money. While he went on occasional vacations and spent time with his family prior to this revelation, after reading the book, his perspective changed. He wanted to invest his money with more observation and intentionality. Now, he's planning trips with his family with more purpose, he's still working because he loves what he does, and he's giving back to people in need. He's expanding his horizons and continuing to grow as a person.

There is so much more to life than money. I believe that success for a wealthy person includes a multitude of memory royalties that you share with other humans, that your people will remember you for the ways that you were intentional. We have to shift our perspective from viewing wealth accumulation as the main goal, or worse—the only goal. Memory royalties are an investment into a richer life and into meaningful relationships. We have to retrain our brains to care about more than a big bucket of money at the end of the road—to care about memories, too.

Creating memories takes time, and we can use our money to create more of it. The concept "money is tokenized time" is somewhat complex (it was for me, anyway), so I've dedicated an entire chapter to it.

That chapter is coming up next.

CHAPTER 4

Money Is Tokenized Time

*"In this world, with great power
there must also come great responsibility."*
—UNCLE BEN, *Spider-Man*

WHEN I WAS A KID (OKAY, MAYBE STILL), SPIDER-MAN was my hero. I collected comic books and, especially when times were tough, I'd pull out Spider-Man and read it to remind me that someone could be born normal but still become extraordinary (by a freak accident, mind you). I thought maybe if I could just get bitten by a radioactive spider, I could save the world too. In those moments, I needed to believe and hope in something.

I also recognized, even then, that Spider-Man had to make all sorts of sacrifices to protect his secret identity. He had to keep his distance from people. He was lonely. This gave me perspective—as good as it sounded to get out of my current situation, the grass wasn't necessarily greener on the superhero side. Spider-Man had great power, but that meant having a heck of a lot more concerns too. But you almost never see Spider-Man bemoaning his great responsibilities to save the world and fight evil. His power was a gift and something he handled with great care, for the good of others.

It's easy to forget how fortunate we are for the power that we have achieved (or been given, in some cases). And it is easy to forget to recognize the great responsibility—not as a burden, but as a gift, one that provides the greatest gift of all: that is, time. It's easy to forget that most people do not have the luxury of time because they are spending their waking minutes working just to survive. If you are lucky enough to be in the top 5 percent, you are lucky enough to have time—precious time—to invest in other people, in memories, and in making our world a better place. Time to be an inspiration.

Buying Time

I turned fifty right before the COVID-19 pandemic, and the reality of being half a century old started to settle in. I say "half a century" because that feels more impactful to me. Halfway to one hundred—I've been around for a while now. Aside from my refusal to *act* fifty (I'm still up to a lot of my twenty-five-year-old antics), this milestone has hit me hard.

I don't know if I'll get another fifty years, and this realization has pushed me to be more intentional, to spend my time more thoughtfully, and to think more critically about my attachments.

At the dawn of my fiftieth trip around the sun, I was in the middle of reading *Knowledge and Power*, a 2013 novel by George Gilder, an incredible futurist, capitalist, and former advisor to Ronald Reagan. Gilder spoke to an idea that money is tokenized time—that we can use money to buy time, which can then be used as a conduit to amplify our experiences, create long-lasting memories, and add fulfillment to our existence, if we let it.

> **Tokenized time,** *noun:* a certain amount of wealth or affluency that provides flexibility in lifestyle to invest in choices that add value, meaning, and joy to your life (i.e., travel, education, experiences, hobbies, etc.).

I recently used some of my own tokenized time to attend an Alder retreat at the Ojai Valley Inn in California, where I joined several friends and clients to listen to many inspiring speakers. The goal of these events is simply to learn: to expand our perspectives, to disconnect from our own bubbles, and to find better ways to address problems. These experiences are unfailingly positive memory royalties for me, ones that compound exponentially over the years.

Two of the speakers were a soon-to-be-married couple, both successful and driven entrepreneurs. They shared thoughts and answered questions about what it looks like for two high-powered, dynamic business people to be in a relationship on a day-to-day basis. It was good for me to see what a successful business *and* personal relationship can look like; this is information I can now share with my clients.

This is an example of how we can use money to invest into an experience that not only creates memories but also broadens our perspective and makes us more open-minded. I got to spend several days with some amazing and inspiring people, and I walked away with new ideas and perspectives that I can share with clients down the road.

The realization that money is meant to do so much more than accumulate has greatly informed the way we at Clarity Capital Partners work with clients and talk about investments. If money is tokenized time, then accumulation applies not only to tangible assets but *also* to memories, ideas, thoughts, relationships, and skills. We want to help coach our clients on how to spend their money, *and* their tokenized time, well.

We put a ton of value on tangible assets, far more than what we put on memory royalties. But these tangible assets—an extra home, another car, a private plane—are liabilities. Not only are they depreciating, they also require time to maintain and utilize. A number of our clients have second homes in Hawaii, for example, and one family hasn't been to theirs in several years. They don't even know what it looks like now! The home is a liability: what are they going to do with it? Do they sell it? Keep it for the kids? Will the kids even want it? Then it becomes their responsibility. Do they rent it out? Will other people ruin it? And there's this constant obligation to plan a trip to Hawaii, even if none of them want to go.

On the other hand, memory royalties don't become a liability and they don't require time to maintain. You can invest in a trip with your family, learn a new skill, or enjoy an incredible meal without ongoing obligation. You just get to go and enjoy it. Your tokenized time can be spent on experiences that don't lose their value. As you put them in your memory vault, they only appreciate over time. They only become brighter as you get older, royalties that bolster you as a person, that build stronger connections with your loved ones, and that make your life richer and more fulfilling. Furthermore, the loved ones who share in these experiences may turn around and do something similar for their inner tribe, planting more seeds that continue to grow and blossom, and providing ongoing value and meaning for generations to come.

The more money you have accumulated, the more tokenized *time* you have. When you have more time, more choices and opportunities come along with it; opportunities for life-changing experiences you'll remember forever. If you are blessed to have affluence, you are also tasked with the responsibility to steward your time well, to think purposefully about where to invest your time in a way that is meaningful and impactful. And—just like Spider-Man's power and influence—this responsibility is an honor and privilege.

Stewarding Time

But here's the catch—more choices does not simply equal more happiness. This is what I often see with our clients and why I am so passionate about partnering with them to discover a more joyful, fulfilling direction. When we don't embrace the reality that money is tokenized time and use it intentionally, graciously, and creatively, we risk stagnation, paralysis from fear, and bitterness. But if we *do* take the time to think about *who we are* and the *imprint* we want to leave behind—our legacy—we can invest in experiences, our inner tribe, and a bright future.

When you consider the legacy you will leave behind, the life you live out in front of your children and grandchildren, it's important to think about your values and how your investments reflect them. You can choose to invest your money in a way that reflects your goals. After you pass away, when your loved ones gather for your funeral, do you want them to celebrate all of the money you accumulated? (I personally have not received a funeral invitation that said, "Please join us for a celebration of Mr. X's money.") Or do you want them to celebrate your life, who you were, what you did, and the legacy you leave behind?

Are you unhappy and afraid of what the future holds?

Or are you investing in memories with your tribe, being generous with what you have, and finding gratitude for life's many gifts?

What sounds more fulfilling?

One of my best friends (and also a client), Aaron, has been an inspiring example for me of this idea of stewarding his time well. A multimillionaire in his early fifties, Aaron has made it a point in his retirement years to get the most out of life, to value experiences over continued accumulation. He invests into diverse memorable experiences and relationships. He's constantly traveling and meeting new people. He's helping his daughter buy her first home in Australia. He sets aside a large sum of money every month just to put toward memory royalties. This means he is actively looking for opportunities to have fun, to learn something new, and to bless the people around him.

Money creates space in your life, time that you wouldn't have if you were working two jobs and frantically trying to make ends meet. Because of this additional time, you have the privilege of contemplating your life, charting your own path, and living intentionally.

Slow Down and Live Fuller

"Sometimes you win, sometimes you ~~lose~~ learn."
—JOHN C. MAXWELL

In 2006, the *Quarterly Journal of Experimental Psychology* included a study that determined time moves faster when you repeat patterns of behavior—when you take the same route to work, eat the same meals, or scroll the same feeds.

What would it look like to do something different every day?

How would it feel to take control of your time by simply switching up the pattern?

Simple variations can remind you you're not stuck, you *can* pursue dreams, and you *do* have the power to make your life better. Variety will also slow time down and remind you to live more mindfully, with intention in each moment.

You could:

- Drive a different way to work or the grocery store (or both).

- Cook something new.

- Quit scrolling and go on a walk.

- Learn a language.

- Learn to code.

- Learn to sing or dance!

Fear often stands in the way of trying new things. The fear of failure. The fear of looking foolish. The fear of quitting. We often tell our clients: Sometimes you win, sometimes you learn! If you can take the thought of "losing" out of the equation, you can view these choices as adventures or growing opportunities. Even if things don't work out the way you hoped, you'll likely learn something about yourself. And if you play out the worst case scenario in your thoughts of trying something new, what is the worst thing that could happen? And what's the best thing that could happen? Don't let fear stand in the way of truly living.

I value the power of choice, of recognizing that I could make decisions for myself. When I was graduating from high school in Missouri, some of my friends couldn't believe that I wanted to go to school in California. They called it "the land of fruit and nuts." *Aren't you scared?* they'd ask me. *You don't know anyone!* But I didn't feel afraid. I felt excited. I was more afraid of the thought of staying in Missouri and doing the same things we'd been doing for the past eighteen years. There's something about making choices, changing things up, and taking control that is empowering and exhilarating. And once you do it a few times, it gets a heck of a lot easier.

This also applies to the way we think. We easily get stuck in repetitive thought patterns without even realizing the same negative or destructive ideas are on repeat. In fact, National Science Foundation research shows that 80 percent of our daily thoughts are negative and 95% are repetitive. Yikes! This type of repetition—especially thoughts that center around how we deserve better or how we have been wronged—gets us stuck in unhelpful ruts.

"My spouse never does *this*."

"Traffic always sucks."

"I have too much to do."

Instead, you can willfully think differently, and sometimes simply having a new thought can add incredible meaning and value to your day.

"My spouse may not do this, but does do *this*."

"Traffic gives me time to disconnect and listen to music or catch up on a podcast."

"This is a great opportunity for me to prioritize."

I often find myself feeling anxious about a speaking engagement or a meeting—but, with a "check myself moment," I realize this is just energy and energy is something I can change, alter, or divert. My next step is to turn that nervousness into excitement for what I will get to share and for the possibility of learning something new! At the Ojai retreat, I moderated a table for generational legacy. I wanted it to be a good experience (and I was definitely nervous about it!). Instead of getting consumed by the pressure, I turned that energy into creativity, and set up the evening as an "Ask Me Anything" (AMA) scenario, inviting everyone at the table to ask each other *any* question. It became an enlightening opportunity to learn from each other.

Thinking differently often requires us to get out of the same physical patterns. If you find that you're succumbing to this "I deserve" attitude or victim mindset, take the time to volunteer somewhere. Some of our clients recently participated in a Christmas gift exchange. They went with their children to buy gifts for a family who was financially struggling during the holiday season. The families sat down together and gave gifts and had real conversations. This was life-changing for all of them. Particularly for the affluent family, it was eye-opening and helped them recognize all they had and the absolute joy of giving.

And this is becoming increasingly important.

With advances in technology, medicine, and the human genome, we are living longer and healthier lives. (Some US doctors predict that if you are alive in 2030, you will likely live to be one hundred years old.) That means you could still be traveling when you're ninety!

So, why should I care at all about turning fifty? (Or turning forty-nine, for that matter.)

Us being healthier and living longer allows us the opportunity to live fuller, richer lives—to see, experience, and know more.

But how can we experience more if we're not willing to spend (or rather, *invest*) our money, instead preferring to keep it locked up in a vault? Money is tokenized time, but only if we let it be. The challenge is to let go of the constraints you have around money and use it to create memory royalties. Investing our tokenized time into memory royalties begins by thinking about our time differently, as a tool that can truly create more value, meaning, and happiness in our lives. That means we not only have to identify the things worthy of our time—we also have to establish space in our schedule to do these things! This will be the topic of our next chapter.

CHAPTER 5

Time Blocking and You

*"Most plans are worthless,
but the process to create a plan is priceless."*
—WINSTON CHURCHHILL

WHEN I WAS GROWING UP, MY DAD TOLD ME, "Todd, with your body type—you're not running from a fight. You can't run, son. You gotta stay and fight."

While he was referring to my shorter, sturdier figure, this has actually proved true for my work ethic as well. I'm not a long distance runner. I'm more of a short sprinter, where I thrive in forty- to fifty-minute focused efforts, with ten-minute brain breaks to refuel, reposture, and get back in the race. Professionally, this model works well in my industry, where I'm able to schedule thirty- to forty-five-minute meetings and buffer on either side to prepare, recover, and wrap up.

It's also led to a natural organization of my days. If you look at my weekly work calendar, you'll see blocks of time allotted to specific tasks: client meetings, email responses, internal research, etc.

However, it took me a long time to realize this same tactic could be implemented toward long-term goals and in my personal life. This realization has been life-changing. It's helped me identify my goals and dreams, solidify the steps to get there, and allot time to invest into these action items. Ultimately, it's held me accountable to live a more purposeful life. And it's certainly freed up space in my schedule for more memory royalties.

I call this time blocking.

What Is Time Blocking?

Time blocking is an empowering exercise to take control of your calendar, reverse engineer your time, and focus on running your own race. By setting annual, quarterly, monthly, and daily goals, you ensure that you devote time to things that matter to you in the moment and that will help you achieve your long-term goals.

> **Time blocking,** *verb:* The act of setting aside chunks of time devoted to single tasks, reverse engineered toward achieving specific, predetermined goals.

Time blocking begins with thinking about the big picture first, by answering the question, "Where do I want to be three to five years from now?" You then consider what it's going to take to get there each year, each month, each week, each day, or each hour. You block off time for these particular activities and set them in place on your schedule, so that you prioritize them and commit *uninterrupted* time to them.

"Uninterrupted" is a key word here. By devoting uninterrupted time—meaning, undistracted, not multitasking, single-focused—the supercomputer inside your head (I'm talking about your brain!) can operate at full capacity. You can get into a "flow," where you experience another level of energy and presence—much like a runner's high has been described—and ultimately increase productivity and decrease fatigue. It's a kind of magic.

While financial and business goals are typically the first things that come to mind, it's equally valuable to consider relational, experiential, and health goals as well—to block off time for family and friends, vacations and entertainment, exercise and meditation. By reverse-engineering your time, you can ensure you invest intentionally and consistently into all of the things that matter to you. Start with your goals and work backward. Then, reevaluate to see if your calendar reflects your goals. This practice can be incorporated into both your professional *and* personal life.

At our office, on a weekly basis, our first priority is interactions with clients. We want to be fully present and actively engaged during our face-to-face meetings throughout the week. Therefore, we devote Mondays and Fridays to "Clarity Days." We block this time off to do all of the other stuff—answer emails, conduct internal research, schedule appointments, strategy development, etc. These are necessary tasks that set us up for time with clients, so we start and close the weeks like this. Then, Tuesdays through Thursdays we are 100 percent available to our clients in-person. (It's important to note that this is our ideal schedule, but we do have exceptions to the rule and obviously interruptions and unexpected needs arise at times.)

In my personal life, I value time with my family, exercise, and being alone. That means I block off time for all of these things. In the past, I'd set aside time for coffee with my daughter, especially when we were on vacation. While on a family trip to Mexico one year, every day, we'd enjoy coffee at the resort's coffee shop. My son and I used to box together (not each other!) every Saturday morning. I make sure I have daily time to read or exercise. I've realized that if it's not on my schedule, it probably won't happen. And at the end of my life, I want to be able to say that I invested into these memory royalties: my health, time with my children, reading great books, and going on trips with my family.

Time blocking will look different for everyone (because we're all running our own race!). The important thing is to identify *your* goals and activities that are joyful and life-giving to *you*, and then work your way backward to ensure your time is spent moving toward those things.

Time Cleanse

Steven Griffith, in his book *The Time Cleanse*, encourages a similar concept. A *time cleanse* is purging your schedule—eliminating anything that doesn't align with your goals. If you start with an end-goal in mind, you then reverse-engineer your schedule and rid it of any activities that interfere or detract from your goal. If your goal is to build your company up to $2 billion assets under management, you could focus on cutting anything from your schedule that doesn't lead to achieving the goal. For example, do you really need to sit in on every internal or operational meeting?

Think about how much time is wasted with distracting notifications, quick one-off emails, and moving into and out of focus on a task because you're pausing to respond to an email. Often this can also lead down a path you didn't mean to travel, stealing precious time that was meant for something else. However, if you allot a certain time during your day to take care of emails (and don't check it otherwise!), you can be hyper-focused on this task alone: reading, organizing, responding, and deleting. You can take control of your time, truly focus, and be far more efficient.

This year, one of my clients wanted to focus on strengthening relationships with his three children. With this in mind, he took a look at his calendar for the year and blocked off evenings and several weekends to ensure he had time set aside for each one of them. He realized pretty quickly that, at ages fourteen, sixteen, and eighteen, it's not necessarily a priority for *them*! I was reminded of a valuable lesson:

sometimes, we have to let ourselves off the hook. Not all of our attempts are going to succeed. Our days are going to get hijacked by emergencies and surprises and urgent needs. We also can't expect others to want and need the same things we do. In this situation, he can continue to block off time for his children, let them know he wants to spend time with them, and be fully present and available to them during those times!

Yes Man

Time-blocking can be used to help source memory royalties, as well. We encourage our clients to schedule time to think and *dream* about experiences they want to have, jot down their ideas, and put plans into motion.

- Where haven't you traveled yet?

- What do you want to see?

- Who do you want to go with?

- What steps will it take to get there?

- Can you set aside time on your calendar to book travel, schedule excursions, and even pack?

As we get better at time blocking, it becomes easier to say *yes* to the right things and *no* to things that are distractions.

We want to move toward cutting out as many things as possible that aren't a "heck yes," to move away from wishy-washy in order to draw out more purpose and passion in all that we do—for every yes to be a "*hell* yes."

One of our clients recently divorced. For ten years, her husband refused to travel with her, even though this was one of her dreams. So in her newfound freedom, one of her primary, non-negotiable goals was to see and experience the world. Soon after the divorce finalized, she planned a solo trip to Dubai and the Maldives. A couple of weeks before the trip, she was talking with a friend. He asked if she was going to scuba dive in the Maldives. She said, "Nope, wasn't planning on it. I'm not a diver." But he insisted she needed to look into it, as the Maldives are one of the best places in the entire world to dive (and very hard to get to).

So she did. Come to find out, the place she was staying is the best place in the country to dive. It felt serendipitous. But here's the thing—this woman had scuba dived once, ever. And this was twenty years prior. She didn't have a certification and in order to get one (in two weeks' time), she would have to dedicate more than twenty hours to e-learning and pool time. She was working insane hours, in the middle of a divorce, and packing up her home! The road to scuba diving certification was not a well-planned path.

But she thought about her goal. She thought, *This is worth it. A once-in-a lifetime opportunity to see the world.* So she said yes, blocked off time, and made it happen.

If she hadn't solidified her goal of traveling and experiencing the world, this yes may have been more difficult. It may not have happened. If she wasn't practicing time-blocking, she may have looked at her schedule and thought, *No way. Can't do it.* But the combination of creating memory royalties and time-blocking made this incredible experience possible for her. And she got to go scuba diving in one of the most beautiful places in the world. For her, this was a *hell yes* opportunity.

Multitasking Is a Myth

One of the biggest benefits of time blocking is focus. While multitasking used to be glorified as a sort of superpower, it's now viewed more and more as an illusion. When you try to do several things at once, you aren't focused on the task at hand. Time blocking helps to eliminate multitasking because you can hone in on one thing at a time.

If you can go to bed at night, knowing you have a plan in place for the next day, knowing that you have time set aside to accomplish the tasks that need to get done, you will likely sleep better at night. You don't need to toss and turn wondering how you're going to get everything done. You have a plan! But—in order to actually accomplish said tasks—you have to set aside all other distractions to focus on what needs to be done. You have to filter out the unnecessary time sucks. These can come in many forms, but one of the sneakiest ways we multitask is through social media and clickbait rabbit trails. I can't tell you the number of times an ad pops up and I travel down a rabbit trail and lose precious time in my day.

Part of eliminating multitasking has to do with reducing the number of decisions we make on a daily basis. Steve Jobs is famous for wearing the same outfit every day (among other things). In fact, he once said he had one hundred of the same black turtlenecks in his closet. His motivation is simple: he doesn't want to allocate attention to picking out his outfits. He wants to use this brain space for more important things. That's not to say you should fill your closet with black turtlenecks, but it is helpful to consider how you can eliminate certain decisions that take your time and energy away from the most important thing—to enjoy life and all it has to offer.

The Time Block Game

At our office, we have a point system to gamify time blocking. Every call or email with a client is worth one point. These take ten to fifteen minutes of our time each day. Face-to-face meetings are five points because they take longer, and there is more preparation and active listening involved. The goal is to get twenty points a day. But we also have extra credit points (for things like responding to a client within a few hours or giving a client a call in response to an email) that encourage our employees to make every day meaningful, to not just go through the motions and do the same things we do every other day.

Part of the "time block game" is to set aside time with no designated activity. That means you can devote this part of your day to whatever you want and need—a mental strategy session, reading a book, going to see a movie by yourself (if you're like me!), sitting outside in the sunshine, whatever! It helps balance your time, eliminate fatigue, use different parts of your brain, and create space for some invaluable (and perhaps spontaneous) memory royalties. This morning, on my way to work, it was 6:00 a.m. and there was a beautiful full moon still out. Because I had the time set aside, I was able to stop and marvel and think about the possibility of life on the other side of the moon!

Time Slippage

"Ravé says that all three pillars—time, attachment, and expectation—have to be present for fear to exist. If you knock down even one of them, fear will get up as that lion did and quietly walk away."
—DAVE ASPREY, *Game Changers*

In the restaurant world, "slippage" refers to the cash your employees skim off the top. It's a little bit, here and there, that adds up over the months and years. It's unaccounted for—a lost opportunity. The same happens with our time, if we don't protect it and spend it intentionally. We get twenty years down the road and wonder...

- Why didn't we accomplish certain things?

- Why didn't we follow up with that person?

- Why didn't we go on that trip?

- Where did all of our time go?

Time blocking can prevent feelings of regret, dissatisfaction, and victimization. Simply put: time blocking can help us find more happiness.

It's not a fix-all, and there will be distractions, emergencies, and interruptions along the way that you can't plan for. But time blocking ensures you put habits into practice that will move you toward your goals. It ensures you allot time for the things that are going to make your life feel meaningful, whether those things are business, family, experiences, health, or something else. All the while, you are also affirming to yourself that you are NOT a victim of the world and your circumstances, that you have incredible amounts of power and plenty of control!

When I was young, it was obvious to everyone that I was a sprinter, not a long-distance runner. I didn't have the build for it! Today, I'm still a sprinter; professionally, and I work best in short bursts, so I time block my schedule accordingly.

Time blocking holds you accountable, not only to accomplish goals and chase dreams, but also to live a meaningful life—to invest time into things that matter to you. To run your own race. To consider more than just accumulation and what you don't have, and truly think about your impact and where you want to spend your invaluable time. It is a hope that, while you are running your own unique race, you may be inspiring and empowering others to do the same.

CHAPTER 6

Detach from Your Attachments

"The business of life is the acquisition of memories.
In the end that's all there is."
—BILL PERKINS, *Die with Zero*

NELSON MANDELA WAS FORTY-FOUR WHEN HE FACED a life sentence in prison, for charges that were later overturned. He spent twenty-seven years behind bars before he was released in 1990. Four years later, he was sworn in as the first President of South Africa.

If Mandela's goal was to become a leader for his country, one could argue that he was detached from a specific path to get there. He could have given up when he was sentenced to life in prison—who could be a leader from a prison cell?—but he didn't. He had faith, grit, and determination. He was steadfast because he seemingly wasn't attached to a specific path, only to the end result.

During volatile markets (both positive and negative), we at Clarity Capital have to be steadfast with our clients. Bear and bull markets come and go, and we want our clients to feel relaxed through any market swings, high or low. Ups and downs are all learning experiences, and we encourage our clients to detach from the results.

Paradigm Shift

I used to have the biggest attachments to arbitrary milestones—achievements or numbers or to-dos—that I was convinced I should have already completed. Most of this was determined by comparing my life to friends or acquaintances. Things like: *Why am I not further along in my career? Why am I not semi-retired? Why are we not managing $10 billion in our firm? Why haven't I written a book yet?*

I was looking at other people's journeys and becoming attached to *their* race, and therefore losing sight of the abundance that was right in front of me. When I listened to the WWII veteran speak about his own, unique experience—not getting married, choosing to travel alone, pouring his life into helping other people with PTSD experience healing—I realized his detachment was true freedom. He was on his own journey, he was owning that, and he was happy and content and peaceful.

I realized that the only way to experience this amount of freedom was to let go of these attachments. This wasn't a physical release, but a paradigm shift. I realized that I couldn't keep measuring my life based on other people's expectations or experiences. And that the picture I had in my head of my life and achievements, the expectations I had put on myself, weren't serving me. And if everything turned out the way I thought it would, how boring would that be?!

So I gradually started thinking differently, recognizing the moments I was obsessing over my own portfolio, my own assets, my own ridiculous "destinations." I started looking for opportunities to celebrate my friends and their accomplishments, rather than letting those things become a reflection of what I hadn't yet done. I started to be more and more inspired by people accomplishing their dreams, and I got to add these celebrations to my own store of memory royalties! Because those experiences change *my* DNA—to see people I love succeeding is inspiring and reinforces all that is possible.

REACTIVE BEHAVIOR

When we are too attached to our portfolio, we struggle to ride the waves of fluctuation. When the market is down several days in a row and the media is telling us to be afraid, we do a few calculations and go into a panic because we're projecting our losses (usually also inappropriately expediting and extrapolating them—that this is happening *right now!*)

and thinking that everything we've ever dreamed of isn't going to happen.

We lose sight of the bigger picture because we're too attached to the immediate. And we react, often by cashing out or changing directions altogether. At the very least, we lose sleep or waste our treasure of time worrying too much.

It is important to frame our fearful moments in these times. Selling out and shifting to cash is the first decision, but with this choice comes a second, intricately linked decision: When will we get back in the market? When do we invest again?

You can either ride the wave or sell and cash out, which also means deciding whether or not to invest again and *when* (usually after the market has bounced). To ride the wave, we can objectively look at our time horizons to determine whether they are skewed. Or we can evaluate whether we've been properly prepared. Ideally, charts and graphs slope upward and to the left, signifying a steady upward trajectory. But unfortunately, this is on paper, not in life! If you were to look at a chart or graph of the market over the last ten, twenty, or fifty years—you would see a whole lot of zigs and zags!

One of our clients decided to cash out during the 2016 elections. He said, "I don't want to be in any kind of financial securities with the 2016 election on the horizon." He was willing to take the tax hit and be a hundred percent in cash. Then—the market moved up soon after President Trump got elected. And for the following four months, the market continued opening up. By the time he was ready to get back in, he had taken some realized losses, missed a lot of the gain from the market bounce, and was facing a tax consequence too!

By this, I mean return to your end goals. Try to detach yourself from the initial emotional response—panic or fear or worry—and observe the situation from above. What are my objectives? Are these still my ultimate goals? How soon do I need this money? For instance, if the goal is to pay for your child's college education and they are eighteen years old (and just a few years away), it may not be a bad idea to move to a more conservative allocation. It's probably not a great idea to risk that money (and likely you should have been more conservative before the downward jolt). But if that goal is still fifteen years down the road, then you have a long time horizon, and patience will likely serve you here. Get factual about your decision, take control, breathe, and assess based on your goals.

If you've anchored yourself too much to your portfolio, you're living in this state of reactivity far too often. The market being up does not mean that our plans are "right." Nor does the market being down imply that our plans are "wrong." There is no straight line from a low point to a higher point on any market graph and, given enough time, these short-term extreme gyrations smooth themselves out.

WORK WITH YOUR TEAM

The bigger picture is this: the market cannot be up every day, nor can life, and when we look at a historical chart, we're not looking at a straight line. A chart rarely goes parabolic up or down for an eternity. So, while you *can* get a scorecard every day, daily marks won't necessarily correlate to your long-term goals. Your financial team can help you respond to market fluctuations in a detached way, rather than reacting out of fear.

Your team can also help you diversify your portfolio so it includes non-correlated assets and helps you strike a delicate balance. It's like a garden, where some flowers take off and others take more time. We don't necessarily uproot these struggling flowers—we try to figure out what they need. We fertilize and water and wait to see what happens. Non-correlation does not mean that absolutely everything in your portfolio will be doing the same! While we can't guarantee that the market won't get worse, we do know that if we stretch your horizon out, it becomes less and less likely.

As a private client boutique firm, Clarity offers our clients an evolving perspective. Meaning, we are constantly learning and growing. First and foremost, we listen to our clients and ask what they want to get out of our meetings. Because we have worked with so many different families, we have gleaned priceless wisdom from their stories. We often help our clients move out of paralysis, observe the facts, and make decisions based on their long-term goals and lifestyle desires. We simply don't get wrapped up in the emotional aspects of the market, and we are here to listen, to take temperature checks, and to offer advice based on real-life stories and experiences.

MATERIAL ATTACHMENT

We also often see this sense of futile attachment in regard to tangible things. One of our clients is a car guy—he measures his days by whether his car is running well or not. He recently purchased an aftermarket tuner for an older Corvette, and it wasn't working properly. He couldn't stop talking about it—he couldn't believe someone would sell him a faulty tuner kit. It ruined his day, maybe even his week. It's been months, and he may still be talking about that tuning kit!

But do you see what's happening here? We get attached to things—whether it's a car or a house or a portfolio— and we let these things determine our moods, outlook, and openness to life. And instead of jumping on opportunities to create memory royalties, enjoy the things we *do* have, and engage in meaningful conversations, we cling to our assets and focus on the "lack." Ultimately, this perpetuates negativity and "victim speak" because of things that we cannot actually control.

QUANTITY VERSUS QUALITY?

I see this often with how clients view time with their children. They get *attached* to the experiences themselves, to creating the next big wow factor for their kids. In the meanwhile, they miss out on the everyday memory royalties that happen just by being fully present. We focus so often on quality time and forget that quantity can matter more to a child. Spending time every day with our children is likely more important than taking them on an epic vacation once a year.

Memory royalties are not limited to epic adventures. They can be as simple as dinner with your children at the kitchen table, walking around the block, or—for me—pranking or scaring your kids on random occasions! These daily, sometimes spontaneous memories require presence. If you choose to be in the moment, you can take advantage of opportunities like these. Think about how these moments build on each other, add value to your days, help change up the monotony, and deepen your relationships—they are invaluable. The best part is they don't require months of planning, expensive plane tickets and hotels, or even leaving your own home!

SHIFTING THE FOCUS

The Rolling Stones put it perfectly when they wrote lyrics about getting what you want versus what you need. We often confuse our wants and our needs, and this can amplify our attachment to material things. We start to think that we need *this* much money in our bank account. We need the *latest* version of our car. We need a *second* home in the Bahamas. But if we can take a step back and recognize all of these things as *wants*, we can create space to detach, let go of control, and find freedom. While we may *want* all of these things, we likely have everything we need to live a happy and comfortable life. What we really *need* is to change our perspective.

Maybe this means adopting a practice of gratitude, acknowledging all of the goodness in your life. Maybe it means letting go of control by turning off the TV, resisting checking the market every day, and riding the waves of fluctuation (in the market and life!). Maybe it means investing more money (a.k.a. tokenized time) on memory royalties instead of focusing purely on material accumulation. The beauty is that change, in this case, happens internally, with your mind, which is something you absolutely have control over!

There are endless choices of things to do that will add value to your life and take your focus off the things you can't control. Trying to control the stock market or real estate market is a fool's errand: it isn't possible. But investing time into learning a new skill, walking, enjoying coffee with a friend, gardening, or reading a good book creates memory royalties that are priceless and don't cost large sums of money! Diversifying where you spend your time and attention also helps you to detach from the things that you can't control.

While you can't control the market, you can control what you invest your tokenized time into. And, unlike physical assets, memory royalties don't deteriorate with age and will hopefully bring a smile to your face (even those bad ones can make you laugh down the road!) or tears to your eyes. They make you *feel*. You can choose which ones you want to repeat or alter or avoid! You can plant your own garden of experiences and it can look however you want it to. So, as you detach from things you can't control, you free up more time and energy to pour into the experiences you can mold and cultivate.

MAKING THE CHANGE

The story I shared about the World War II vet at the beginning of the book absolutely altered the way I viewed attachments. This man's ability to detach himself from dramatically damaging and negative experiences to rise up and move made me look at my life differently. It highlighted areas where I had an unhealthy attachment, including my financial situation. It made me realize that if this veteran could pivot, could detach from some monumental experiences in order to move forward and live a meaningful life, very certainly I could do the same. My fear of losing my business or all of my wealth was *nothing* in comparison to what this man had to overcome. If he could change, I could too.

I took some time to consider the worst case scenario—for me, that meant envisioning my company going to zero, my entire family not having food on the table, and everyone seeing me as a failure or fraud because I didn't see something that came around a corner. Or any number of other things—getting divorced, some random accident for my kids, or having my reputation destroyed.

Every single one of these things—whether it's a failed company or nuclear war—are ultimately out of my control.

The amount of time and energy wasted on worrying and projecting, on fearing and complaining, is alarming. Even if one of these things happened, I would figure it out. I would do what I needed to do to get through it, to protect my loved ones, and to continue living. What have I actually gained by trying to control them now?

ACTIVELY DETACH

Instead of continuing down this path of futile attachment, I want to invite you to detach from the things you cannot control. How? Take a breath. Pull yourself outside of the mind-chaos and remind yourself that there's nothing you can do about most of these things. Then, focus on the things you do have control over. Do one thing—big or small—that reinforces the fact that you are in control of some things. Turn off the news. Make your bed. Exercise. Eat something healthy. Call a friend. Meditate.

This takes time and practice. And it's not easy (if it were easy, everyone would be doing it!). You have to actively shift the way you think. So when you find yourself spiraling into panic or fear, *choose* to refocus (often over and over and over again!). There's no need to beat yourself up or shame yourself for returning to old thought patterns. Instead, remind yourself that you have the power to choose. You can choose to be happy, to be powerful, to be open-minded, to change it up, to invest your time into something else, something that serves you.

We can also let go of our attachment to particular outcomes. This is especially apparent when it comes to memory royalties. We often plan trips hoping and thinking they will be mind-blowing or a cure for hard times or an incredible bonding time for our families. We put a lot of pressure on these experiences to look and feel a certain way. But if we are to approach our memory royalties with an open-handedness, unattached to a particular outcome, we can experience more freedom and surprises along the way. We can then see negative or less-than-perfect experiences as equally valuable because of what we saw and experienced, and the fact that we learned something new (good or bad!).

FREE TO RUN

"When you're ready to lose your life, you live it. But if you're protecting your life, you're dead."
—ANTHONY DE MELLO and J. FRANCIS STROUD, *Awareness*

Detachment also encourages us to run our own race. If we are attached to our lives looking a certain way—perhaps like a neighbor or some random celebrity or even our parents—we can't actually decipher our own individual path. If we're consumed with other people's benchmarks and reflections, it becomes increasingly difficult to uncover our own passions, dreams, and unique legacy.

This is especially common with our clients who have inherited money. This often gets mixed with a sense of guilt or obligation: *It's not my money. What would my dad or mom want me to do? I don't deserve this.* In this scenario, freedom to operate outside of other people's thought processes and desires is limited. This again comes back to detachment: striking the balance between honoring a previous person's legacy while still remaining true to an individual, personal, whole-hearted journey.

Taking the time to evaluate your personal attachments and to release those that aren't serving you is an incredible way to open up space in your life for more memory royalties. Which means you might find yourself with more time to play with. What will you do with this freedom? How will you spend your precious tokenized time? In the next chapter, we'll talk about just that.

CHAPTER 7

Family Dynamics, Position Sizing, and Diversification

"Strong opinions, loosely held."
—PALO ALTO'S INSTITUTE FOR THE FUTURE

KEVIN AND REBECCA ARRIVED FOR THEIR FIRST meeting with our team as most of our clients do—with plenty of tokenized time and a general sense of how they wanted to diversify and position their portfolio. I began (as I most often do) by asking questions about their long-term goals, non-leading questions that help me understand their priorities and goals.

When I asked, "What are you hoping to accomplish?" The conversation turned into a discussion about family dynamics—specifically about their three children—and I'll be honest, I wasn't the least bit surprised.

This is what we uncovered: their oldest child was a bit of a mess. Their hope was to provide him enough money to get on his feet, but little enough that he would have to develop his own grit, to actually do something with his time and life, to pave his own way. Their second child was the most responsible, the intended executor of their will down the road. He was finishing up a master's degree, already married, making great money, and likely to provide their first grandchild soon. Their youngest—and only girl—was driven to be a veterinarian. They were paying for vet school, planned to cover her wedding (if that was in the cards), and knew she would be good to go from there.

After a lengthy discussion about *family dynamics*, I had a pretty clear picture of how they wanted to allocate their money. And this all began with a question about long-term goals. This isn't uncommon. In fact, most of our long-term goals—if we have children and grandchildren—revolve around our families and their futures. We want to provide. We want to empower. We want our kids to succeed, to be set up well, and to pave their own way in the world. We want to play a part in that, but we typically don't intend to impede their growth.

This is all part of the wealth management conversation. Crazy, huh?

Our clients show up with all of these different dynamics at play, and they want a plan that reflects their goals and takes all of these varying people and needs into account. At our firm, we embrace this as part of our job. Therefore, we ask questions, actively listen, and gather data. We try not to muddy the waters with our financial jargon or straight numbers. And we come up with a plan—*in partnership* with our clients. But we truly believe that we have to understand the underlying dynamics in order to reverse engineer, position size, and diversify for each and every one of our very different clients.

This is a balancing act, and one that we encourage our clients to hold loosely, be flexible with, and adjust as families shift and needs change.

Support and Empower

A good friend of mine, Mike, embodies the Palo Alto Institute for the Future's concept. He has strong ideas about how to plan for future memory royalty curation but isn't held to them—he is open-minded and willing to meet his family where they are.

Mike has inspired me in the way he diversifies his portfolio, particularly when it comes to his children. Mike has three daughters, and he has a financial "bucket" designated for each one. These buckets have changed and morphed as his three girls have gotten older, gotten jobs, and eventually when they get married and have children of their own.

His oldest daughter is a nurse in New York City. He's helping her invest in real estate there and has set up an account for her where she can invest each month. That way, she's building up assets outside of her 401(k).

His middle daughter is living in Australia and wants to start a wine business. He's helping her buy a home and giving her seed money to get her business off the ground.

Mike's third daughter is finishing college, and he's helping her with tuition and cost of living. When she graduates and gets established, Mike will evaluate how he can support her, as well.

Mike has also set up a family dynasty trust for his family, where they all get to decide where to donate money each year. In other words, he's created a "family bank" where they can work together to shape the investments and philanthropic endeavors they pursue, *together*—more memory royalties!

The point is: each daughter is different—their stage of life, their passions, their interests. So he encourages each one of them to curate memory royalties and run their own race, offering guidance and support along the way. Mike doesn't pressure them to be him, to make the same choices he would, or to invest tokenized time the same way. His way of doing this includes setting them up for success, giving them some money (but hopefully not "too much" that would interfere with their journey of "grit"!), and encouraging them to find their own places to invest time and energy.

Meet Them Where They Are

This is easier said than done, of course. We often, particularly with family members, approach these sorts of situations with strings attached and our own baggage trailing behind us. In theory, we want our loved ones to run their own race, as long as it doesn't affect our own, bring hardship into our lives, squander our hard-earned money, make us uncomfortable, or look too far-off from the picture we had of their future!

Mike wasn't *happy* about his middle daughter's choice to live so far away. He wasn't excited, necessarily. And because of this, he could have let her know that he would be glad to help her buy a home, as long as it was within biking distance of his own house. He could have put parameters and requirements on her inheritance. But instead (after some good, long conversations), he chose to invest in her and her personal journey.

This is where the magic happens. When we can detach ourselves from our family members' paths and decisions, we can more easily approach conversations as an active listener. And when we choose to be an active listener, we can actually find understanding—and therefore solutions—quicker. We meet people where they are, meaning we don't expect them to be in the same place we are, and we seek to discover where they actually are on their own journey.

Here's the thing: unmet expectations usually lead to upset. Particularly when they are unspoken or unfair. And particularly when it comes to family members. To expect our loved ones to run the same race, to value the same things, to make the same choices as you are all unfair expectations. Taking the time to listen, to share, and to find common ground is a worthy pursuit...and one that takes intentional time.

To do this well, we start with the idea of position sizing.

What Is Position Sizing?

From a financial standpoint, when we—Clarity advisors—look to develop a portfolio for clients, we examine a combination of factors: age, risk tolerance, invading portfolio for distributions, and what goals they have. Then, we look at it similar to baking a cake; we identify the right recipe, find the ingredients, and put them all together in the right order and amounts. We include our clients in conversations throughout the entire process, so that we can cover pros and cons of each option, and we also typically offer some empirical anecdote about what another family or client has done (again, with the goal of making only new mistakes).

For instance, imagine you are thrilled about investing into the world of EV cars in China. Right now, there are something like 250 electric vehicle companies in China. If this was the path you chose, our advisors would want to position size your investment in order to control risks and maximize returns. Say we decide to allocate between 5 and 10 percent of your portfolio to electric vehicles. We, as your wealth managers, would then determine the biggest electric car companies, the ones that have control of some of the market share. We would likely allocate more to these companies—say, 80 percent of the allocation. The remaining 20 percent of your allocation would go into some smaller, riskier, nascent companies that offer something unique and desirable, like a quick-charge option, or a lightweight battery, or a hydrogen electric combination.

POSITION SIZING FOR YOUR FAMILY

How do we then utilize this idea of position sizing within the realm of family dynamics? At Clarity, we start with the same idea—control risks and maximize returns—when it comes to creating buckets and allocating investments for your family members.

Every single family is different, so there isn't a one-size-fits-all package that we offer (and thank God there isn't... how boring!). We truly value getting to know each of our clients, understanding their unique goals, and spending a lot of time just listening and uncovering priorities, hopes, and passions. Typically, we compare total family investments to those big companies that have control of the market—these are where you'll likely get the most bang for your buck. Investing a big portion of tokenized time into experiences that impact your entire family usually return an enormous investment from memory royalties.

Another option (there are endless possibilities) for this bigger bucket is to create a family foundation or family dynasty trust, like my buddy Mike. This is a type of trust that allows you to pass wealth from generation to generation with tax advantages. This big bucket can then pour into individu-alized, smaller buckets, perhaps for each family member or various causes. But all of these buckets align with the overall family's legacy, goals, or dreams.

These smaller buckets, or smaller position sizes, would pertain to each individual family member. You might have a bucket for each kid, based on their age and pursuits in life. You might have buckets for yourself, your spouse, or the two of you together. We recognize that each client is running their own race, that people have differing opinions on colleges, trusts, seed money, second homes, etc. There's a number of ways to allot the money in these buckets.

Another position sizing option for your children is called a spendthrift trust. Instead of a beneficiary receiving their access to funds all at once, the money is released incremen-tally, sometimes after certain milestones are achieved, like finishing college or securing a job or getting married. This is a great way to allow your children to run their own race, while still ensuring that they are mature and responsible enough to invest their inheritance well.

At Clarity, we want to meet our clients where they are at. We absolutely will crunch numbers for you. But first and foremost, we want to hear from each individual: What are you trying to achieve? While we can throw out ideas and offer advice, the most important thing is to understand the end goal and reverse engineer from there. If your goal is to save enough money, over the course of twenty years, to send each one of your children to college, we would invest differently than if your goal is to skip out on kids and travel multiple times every year.

POSITION SIZING YOUR TIME

This same concept applies to your time as well. We want you to invest the most time, money, and thought into the memory royalties that are going to increase fulfillment and happiness in your life. If you decide that vacations with your family are a top priority, we might suggest you allocate 80 percent of your time to a few trips each year. Then, we would advise you to work with the other 20 percent to determine what to do with the rest of your time. The hope is to spend the most time doing things that get you the *best* return on investment— family time, learning a new skill, doing a hobby, etc.

Position sizing your time means you get to intentionally craft your life. You get to take the entire pie and divide it as you like, evaluating and re-evaluating these time investments and changing them up as you see fit. There's no right or wrong, and ideally, it looks different for you than it does for your neighbor, because you are each running your own race.

CARPE DIEM

It's interesting to note a couple of things regarding time investments. We have a tendency to put certain things off, to save big trips or learning a new skill or picking up a new hobby for another day. We claim we're too old or too busy or just too stuck in our ways! However, there's something to be said for the compound interest (remember that concept?) that these memory royalties accrue.

Think about it: if you take your kids (or grandkids) on a memorable, life-changing adventure when they are in their teens, they get to experience and remember that trip—potentially—for the next eighty years! They'll be able to share this with friends and their kids and their grandkids, and this memory royalty lives on, accruing the good kind of interest that impacts generations. As opposed to waiting until your kids are in their fifties, or your grandkids are fully grown, when the transformative potential and the longevity diminishes and the possibility of repeating or building upon it becomes less likely because—simply put—there's just not as much time.

This is maybe a roundabout way of saying: why wait? Or what are you waiting for? We aren't getting any younger!

Diversifying Your Life Portfolio

Diversification, in the finance world, means investing in different assets that are uncorrelated. Think about it this way: if you're cooking a spicy dish for dinner, you probably don't want to add the same amount of jalapeños as you do chicken. You might not end up with the best meal. You want to work toward a nice ratio, where the flavor of the jalapeños is complementary and not overpowering. The same idea applies to investments. We want diverse allocations to try to balance it all out. Meaning, we probably wouldn't encourage you to allocate all of your investments to the EV industry in China. Perhaps in addition to your Chinese EV auto investments, you also allocate some money into the fintech market. The hope being that when one zigs, the other zags. When one investment is down, the other might be up!

In the finance world, if you have a fully diversified portfolio, you likely have an investment (or two) that makes you a little uncomfortable.

The same is true for a diversified *life* portfolio. This goes back to the idea of changing it up, creating new neural pathways, and slowing time down by choosing different roads. Imagine going on the same vacation every year, with the same people, for the same duration of time. Imagine staying in the exact same Airbnb, sleeping in the same bed, and doing the same activities year after year. After a while, these vacations would blur together.

Now, imagine changing it up every year. Going to a different destination, with different scenery and activities, for varying lengths of time. Maybe this seems risky, but it also increases the probability of an amazing, life-changing, notable experience with your family. The participants will talk about this experience. They'll be able to remember that year we went to the Galapagos or Antarctica, what they saw and learned, what the food tasted like, and what ridiculous creatures they encountered.

This idea of diversification applies to daily life, too— looking for opportunities to engage in new experiences for both you and your family members. Finding hobbies or activities that you can share with your family—like weekly dinner dates with a child or cooking classes with your spouse, going to see a musical or trying a new exercise class—these are things that increase your chances of incredible memory royalties, rounding out your life portfolio.

Sometimes You Win, Sometimes You Learn

"How do you define wisdom? Understanding the long-term consequences of your actions."
—ERIC JORGENSON, JACK BUTCHER, and
TIM FERRISS, *The Almanac of Naval Ravikant*

When a risky financial investment hits, it feels incredible. Similarly, some of these *time* investments might make you feel uncomfortable at first. Maybe it's traveling to a location that feels outside of your comfort zone, with a language you don't understand, or learning a skill that intimidates you. In the end, even if it's not a *perfect* experience, you will probably walk away feeling accomplished, satisfied, and proud. More so than if you had simply done something that felt safe and comfortable. These then become experiences you want to do again, no questions asked.

And like with financial investments, not all of your time investments will pan out. You will likely walk away from some experiences thinking, *I'm not going to do that again.* But that doesn't mean you should stop trying new things.

Figuring out what works and what doesn't is all part of the process.

When I was in high school, I thought I'd learn how to play the acoustic guitar so I could meet more girls. Within a few weeks of beginning this pursuit, while I loved listening to music, I realized that I wasn't quite accessing the effortlessness that other musicians seemed to embody when they were strumming their chords. My creative juices refused to flow. So, after weeks of struggling to master "Rolling on a River" by Creedence Clearwater Revival, I decided to give it up, sparing any future victim listener (you're welcome!).

Here's what I learned: it was a lot of work. I would have had to allocate a ton of time to figure it out, to be the cool, skilled guitar-playing guy that I envisioned. More importantly, I learned that I would rather *write* the songs. I'm more of a behind-the-scenes kind of person. I also gained a tremendous amount of respect for musicians—it was not as easy as they made it look! Not to mention, I needed a new way to pick up the ladies.

I don't have regrets about the weeks I "wasted" on learning the guitar. I learned so much. Nothing ventured, nothing gained. The same is true of our portfolio. As we venture to diversify our memory royalties, we're going to learn from each one of them—positive and negative. If we're willing to try new things, to learn from these less-than-ideal situations, we're going to gain a tremendous amount of knowledge, perspective, and direction.

Even when new experiences fail, for you or your family, they are still valuable. It's like dating—sometimes figuring out what you *don't* want is just as valuable as determining what you do. Maybe you go on a cruise with your family and realize that you get seasick. This is important knowledge that can inform your future memory royalties! But just because you had a less-than-ideal experience on the cruise doesn't mean you shouldn't rent a house on the coast with your family *next* summer.

Mike's middle daughter, for example, may decide she doesn't want to stay in Australia and instead move back to the United States to be closer to family. Will that mean her time spent in Australia, or the money Mike spent on the house, will be wasted? No! That money gifted her the time to experience more of her life in Australia. What invaluable memory royalties!

If we have a bad experience, we have the opportunity to observe it, note what we didn't like, and change either our perspective or the experience itself. Our ability to adapt is a superpower. Observation can help us move toward the realm of self-actualization, a deeper understanding of life, and a higher purpose. If we do the same things over and over again, we aren't challenging ourselves to grow. If we experience life through different lenses, constantly challenging ourselves to adapt and shift, we have the opportunity to deepen our own selves and our understanding of the world.

My experience trying the guitar makes me laugh now. While it wasn't a success, it's certainly an entertaining memory royalty for me now! Having ventured down that path in my youth also makes me more open to similar experiences in the future.

Maybe I'll take up the electric guitar or piano!

Maybe I just need some voice lessons!

Needless to say, and thankfully, my motivations have matured. Rather than trying to meet some girls, I would pursue these skills to expand my mind, gain new perspectives, and connect with more people. Currently, as I work on this book, the Clarity Team is creating a song together (moderated by Tiffany Thompson from Alder (formerly Gen Next)—amazing!)—a beautiful memory royalty that will mean something to us as a team.

One thing that I encourage my team to do when discussing memory royalties with our clients is to use critical thinking skills. More on that next.

CHAPTER 8

Critical Thinking

"Be who you are and say what you feel, because those who mind don't matter and those who matter don't mind."
—DR. SEUSS

O UR FIRM BELIEVES IN HELPING CLIENTS THINK critically, not just about their finances, but about how they can live a meaningful and fulfilling life. For many, this is a process of introspection, and we make it a point to help our clients embark on this valuable journey.

Deborah came into the office a few weeks ago with a new 'do. I noticed immediately because this is a woman who emphatically clings to predictability and negativity—a real life Debbie Downer! Deborah—much like many of our clients—was afraid of change and afraid of taking risks. She had lost her husband several years ago, and had been dragging her feet on spending money, despite our assurances that she had more than enough to live the rest of her life in comfort. I complimented her purple highlights (is that a thing?) and asked her what was on her mind.

To my surprise, she said, "I want to go to Texas for a while, to see if there's a place there I'd like to live." I resisted the urge to do a small victory dance, and we proceeded to talk through a game plan with her. We mapped out different places for her to visit based on her lifestyle and desires. I then advised her not to sell her place in California until she had experienced the nuances of Texas living and determined whether this could be a forever move (something many of our clients have learned the hard way).

After she left the office, I went ahead and *did* my little victory dance. Deborah was diversifying her portfolio! She was pursuing memory royalties! She was going to change it up, do something for herself, and take steps toward a more meaningful, enjoyable life.

For Deborah, this process took some time, and it started with planting seeds. Right after her husband passed away, we wanted to help her find a baseline for this new chapter of life. We started by doing a thorough review of her finances and establishing generated income and various "buckets" in her portfolio. While her husband's health had been deteriorating for some time, the finality of his passing was still incredibly painful and disorienting for her. Therefore, she needed to grieve, process, and accept her new reality.

When Deborah started talking about the possibility of moving to Texas, we wanted to encourage and help her in the process of consideration. A lot of wealth management companies wouldn't necessarily advise their clients to spend more money (because that ultimately means less money for them to manage), but our hope is to see our clients live happy and fulfilling lives. If moving to Texas was going to create new and more abundant memory royalties for Deborah, we wanted to help her make it happen!

She came to us asking—from a purely financial standpoint—if she could afford to move. It was an easy answer: yes. But first, we encouraged Deborah to take some time to explore Texas, to bring a trusted friend, drive around some neighborhoods, envision a life and future there. We also invited her to consider renting a home in Texas for the first year, before selling her home in California and making a permanent decision. This is advice we had gleaned from former clients, who hadn't taken the time to explore, had sold their previous homes too soon, and had regretted these decisions. "Can I afford to do that?" she asked us. We crunched the numbers and told her with confidence, "Yes!"

It took Deborah a while to look at her life through a different prism, to see that she had the courage and the tokenized time (money) to make a change. Ultimately, she was the only one who could think through the impact and vision of this decision to move. But we were able to help her think critically, to consider different options, and ultimately to make a wise and empowering choice that would allow her to multiply memory royalties and run her own race.

What Wealth Managers "Should" Be Doing

Are your wealth managers critical thinkers?

As a fee-based wealth management company, we at Clarity Capital Partners want your money to last longer. If there's zero money in the bank, we lose our business! But our team is committed not only to preserving your wealth— we're also committed to thinking critically about *meaningful* ways for you to invest your money. We do everything in partnership with our clients, offering concepts, allocations, and strategies, thinking through pros and cons, taking the time to know who our clients are and what their goals are. Our hope is to serve our clients for many generations, which means we have to be able to speak to several generations at one time, to understand differing perspectives and to think about ways to offer creative solutions across the board.

When we encourage people to spend money on memory royalties, this means less money for us to manage. However, we honestly view memory royalties as an investment, not an expense. These are experiences that will continue to open new doors, help our clients live more fulfilling lives, and create greater, lasting abundance. As a generational wealth management firm, we also believe that helping our clients balance life will provide more long-term direction and meaning in investments and life, both personally and for generations to come. Our hope is that Clarity will have the privilege to continue working with second, third, and fourth generation families, and to provide a link between generations by enabling memory royalties for everyone.

We often start our client meetings by asking, "What are the top three things you want to get out of our meeting?" This shifts the focus from what we have to offer to what our clients *actually* want to learn. We often get very little of our clients' time during certain seasons of their life, so we strive to be ever-present and active listeners to the things that might be keeping them up at night. We are an open forum and will make ourselves available to address the needs and concerns of our clients.

This line of questioning and conversation also helps us identify the problem that each client wants to solve, in order to connect with our clients and reduce other distracting "noise" in the course of finding a solution. We try to avoid jargon (which our wealth management industry is full of!) in order to meet our clients where they are in a language that has meaning for them. We can crunch numbers (taking the "qualitative" conversation to a "quantitative" testing and proving process) later on!

Often, these conversations lead into memory royalties and family dynamics, which is why these have become important focuses for our team. When I first met with Beatriz two years ago, she shared that she was of German descent, with no family left in the motherland. Her husband had passed away several years prior, and they didn't have children. This eighty-year-old woman owns a multimillion dollar home, has no desire to travel, and has no family to leave her money to. This was a conundrum! "What do you want to do with the money?" I asked her. I was ready to take a deep-dive with her to uncover her priorities, her long-term goals, and her hopes for the future. It was time for me to think critically.

Three Potential Solutions

I realized I needed to get more creative, to dig down deep, and to offer a variety of solutions that were simple, feasible, and truly benefited Beatriz. We eventually discovered she wanted to donate her money to some charities, but needed more time to explore options—which charities? Did she want to give the money directly to the charity? Or actually volunteer her time along with her resources?

Every problem has *multiple* solutions—it's our job at Clarity to uncover the possibilities and then choose the best path. No matter how complicated the situation. I encourage all of my team members to come up with three solutions to every problem so they learn how to think critically and not just jump on Google to find the "right" answer. It takes more critical thinking to establish a third option, because you have to come up with something that isn't only the opposite of the first option—you have to come up with something completely different.

Unfortunately, we tend to focus on the negative aspect of the problem. We tend to fall into the trap of thinking we're stuck—*I'm too old, there's not enough time, I could never do that*—and trade possibilities for complacency.

I often tell my team, "Complaining is draining." This is a mantra in our office. Complaining doesn't move us toward solutions—it makes us feel like victims, where we don't take ownership of our problems. Looking for and finding solutions moves us toward gratitude, optimism, and general happiness.

Instead of this outlook, what if you saw *choices*? When you face a difficult issue, take time to critically think about it and write down three possible solutions. This will help you feel less stuck, because you will easily see there are *multiple* options available to you. In a way, this situation, as difficult as it may be, is happening *for* you and not necessarily *to* you. When you partner with our firm, you also get the advantage of all of the other experiences we can translate and transfer to you from our other clients. This will help other choices float to the top (some that you might not have thought about!), choices that are based on *other* people's memory royalties, that can then inform and motivate yours.

We are constantly learning from others' memory royalties! Through friends and family members, through books and movies, through our own experiences—both good and bad. All of these events and perspectives can help us realize how many options there really are and that so much is possible, if we just take the time to consider solutions. Then, we think about pros and cons for each one, and ultimately choose a path that aligns with who we are: we run our own race!

If we intentionally look for areas where we can grow and improve, it alleviates the temptation to focus on lack. Difficult situations aren't simply things to endure—they are often opportunities for growth and self-improvement. But if we *only* choose to see the hard and the bad, we won't realize the good.

Get off the Beaten Path

Realizing the good often means taking a road less traveled. We live in an age where we are spoon-fed information. Whether it's the type of higher education you should pursue, the trip you just need to go on, or what new outfit you *must* have, we encounter a constant infiltration of information that may or may not serve us. This is where critical thinking is crucial.

Healthy skepticism plays a part in this. If you receive an email that promises "You'll look twenty years younger if you take this vitamin once a day," that's worth questioning. If you see a newsletter that promises to "protect your portfolio for life," you might want to do a little sleuthing. If it sounds too good to be true, it probably is! Frankly, what in life is "set it and forget it"? And, if there was something that you *could* set and forget, how boring would that be?!

The next time you find yourself walking a well-worn path toward consumerism or obligation, or observing the lack in your life, take a moment to truly consider whether whatever you're walking toward is something you want and need.

- What would it look like to choose a different direction?

- For your grandchild to go to trade school instead of a university?

- For you to take your family on a service trip instead of a yacht vacation?

Most importantly, don't forget to ask yourself...

- *What do you actually want?*

This question may lead you to discover that you want more out of life. It reinforces that other paths are possible and allowable, that you can try something different. This realization can be incredibly empowering and can help you access a deeper sense of self. You are more powerful, more capable, more flexible than you realize. Maybe answering this question leads you to learn a new skill or acquire a new accreditation. This is an incredible way to continue thinking critically about your life, to realize that you are not at the end of your journey, and that there are almost always ways to continue to grow and learn.

Ten Ideas

James Altucher, author of *Choose Yourself!* and *Skip the Line* (and founder of more than twenty companies), talks about setting aside a time block each day to write down ten ideas. These ideas can be about *anything*—a new business or book idea, date nights with your spouse, recipes, trips, etc. While you likely won't implement all (or any!) of these ideas, it's an incredible practice for your brain that encourages critical thinking, problem-solving, creativity, innovation, and dreaming. In this way, your brain is a muscle and it should get some exercise!

IDEAS FOR INNOVATION TO EXPLORE

The point is to exercise your brain, to encourage yourself to think critically and follow a path that opens up your mind to different possibilities (no matter how random they seem). (Heck, you might make the next big billion-dollar discovery in this simple exercise!) For instance, you might start this process by considering a complete digital world, where we no longer need keys, credit cards, or physical currencies. Your exploration might lead you down a path like this:

1. Keys on the phone?

2. Currency on the phone?

3. Do we short wallet and key makers?

4. Impact on women's handbags?

5. How to transfer the key to the valet?

6. Will driverless cars eliminate physical valet attendants?

7. Impact on parking garages?

8. Will tires last forever?

9. Will ICE engines need mechanics?

10. Service stations for ICE vehicles?

As you engage in this practice, you might notice that certain ideas repeat themselves. Maybe you find yourself incredibly inspired by a particular idea. Maybe you discover that you're excited to explore a new skill. These are things worth paying attention to, as they will lead you to invest your time (and therefore your wealth) in a more meaningful way.

This exercise also helps you connect with childlike wonder; that part of you that looked at the world as a place of possibility, a place where there was *so much* to see and explore. You could be anything! You could *do* anything! Just put on a cape—immediately you are a new, powerful superhero! Even if these ideas are things you don't pursue or don't think about again, you are exercising your brain to remember that there are endless possibilities and different ways to look at your life and circumstances. Every great idea starts *somewhere*, but we have to be willing to think of these ideas first.

As you dive into this practice, you might notice that you are far more open to investing in memory royalties. In fact, you might notice that you start *looking* for opportunities to create different pathways, to develop new skills, to engage in new connections with your loved ones. These ten ideas can lead to a string that you might pull that will then lead to a memory royalty that will then open you up to further empirical knowledge and awareness of possibilities. It's a way to take control of your life and pave your own path.

Only Make New Mistakes

"The only thing I regret about my past is the length of it. If I had to live my life again I'd make the same mistakes, only sooner."
—TALLULAH BANKHEAD

But hopefully, as you think more critically about your time, memory royalties, and problems, you can learn from your mistakes and therefore not make the same ones again! Remember: Sometimes you win...sometimes you...learn!

Now, it's important to note that most people learn more from their mistakes (or "tuition paid") than their successes. Generally, being successful leads to blind spots because we start to think it's easy. We go on autopilot and quit thinking critically. This means that our negative experiences, what we would maybe refer to as "bad memories," are still incredibly valuable. Memory royalties are not just fun, happy, sunny family vacations. They can also be negative experiences that draw us into a deeper understanding of ourselves, help us define our goals, and push us toward the person we want to become.

I tell our clients this often: "We are here to help prevent you from paying tuition twice."

This is another way of saying, "Only make new mistakes," and it certainly pertains to your financial portfolio—you should put trust in a firm that has a history of experience and can pull data from the past to inform choices in the future.

A memory royalty is an investment into ourselves, no matter a "good" or "bad" outcome. That's the beauty of mistakes—you learn. You grow. And then you only make new mistakes in the future, so you can *continue* to learn and grow.

In order to do this, however, we have to take the time to process and explore mistakes; to consider what went wrong, how we would do things differently next time, and how to avoid the same pitfalls. We can't avoid mistakes or failures, but we can change our tune to see these as opportunities to become better, more well-rounded individuals. (This is something Deborah now understands, and she makes conscious decisions to rewire her brain to engage in more positive thinking.)

The ability to only make new mistakes starts with being present and engaged with your life in a way that fosters reflection and therefore growth. Critical thinking is best when combined with feedback. The Feedback Loop is up next.

CHAPTER 9

The Feedback Loop

"The unexamined life is not worth living."
—SOCRATES

WHEN I WAS A KID, I USED TO DO A LOT OF PUZZLES with my grandmother. And every time, I would get impatient with the process. I wanted to see the finished product quickly. I wanted to reverse engineer things and get to the end result. That wasn't really possible—there's no way to do a puzzle except to put one piece in at a time. So inevitably, I'd grow frustrated and my grandmother would say, "Well, let's take a break, and then we can come back and look at this with fresh eyes."

She recognized that we needed to change the scenery a bit, get outside of the situation, and allow for some space.

My dad, on the other hand, wouldn't do this. While he didn't actually participate in the puzzle-making, I can just imagine his response to my frustration: "Buck up, Todd. Rub dirt on it. Figure it out." When I was young (around age fifteen), he gave me a plaque with a duck on it that I still have today. It says, "Always be like a duck. Calm on the surface, but paddling like the devil underneath." He had a brass plaque inscribed for me that says, "To a very special son."

This advice has guided me in many moments: stay calm on the surface, but don't quit hustling to figure it out. A simple memory royalty that has paid huge dividends for me throughout my life's ups and downs—over thirty-five years of compound interest! And this attitude of endurance has enabled me to share this perspective with you, my dear reader, our clients, my team, and maybe more!

These were two of the most influential people in my life, with two very different approaches to difficult situations.

My grandmother: back up, take a breath, re-evaluate.

My father: get back in there, try again, don't give up.

These are two approaches I carry in my back pocket to pull out when the circumstances call for it.

They are also a critical part of the Feedback Loop, a process of learning from experiences in order to inform future decisions, to know when to walk away, and to know when to dig your heels in and keep pressing forward. It's a way to live more intentionally and a way to add incredible value, joy, and growth to your life.

My Feedback Loop consists of six steps:

1. Experience

2. Observe

3. Reflect

4. Implement

5. Move On

6. Find the Silver Lining

Every situation presents an opportunity to learn, but we have to be an active participant. We have to take the time to be present, to examine, and to reflect. And sometimes, in the moment, we have to know when to pause and pull back and when to buck up and get back in the ring.

Step 1: Experience

"The true master arrives without ever having to leave."
—ZEN MASTER QUOTE

Once you've taken the time to think critically about your life, to consider memory royalties, and to block off time, you actually have to take initiative and get in the fight. But I want you to take this one step further—I want to challenge you to be *fully present* in your experiences in order to absorb as much as you can from them.

A few months ago, I was invited to join a client on a trip to Puerto Rico, where he was meeting with a celebrity about purchasing his business. Leading up to the trip, I had to check in with myself. The reality was, I was likely not going to have a full conversation with this celebrity. I'd maybe get thirty seconds of his time, tops. I had to evaluate my expectations and temper them, so that I *could* be fully present. Unmet expectations lead to upset and prevent us from being engaged with reality. I wanted to go into this experience with an open mind, ready to listen and learn. I wanted to show up, unattached to an outcome and untethered to expectations.

The truth is, many of my colleagues would have ducked and run from this experience. This part of Puerto Rico is popular amongst people that make money in digital assets; there's a sort of crypto mafia population there (because of the tax benefits, but that's a story for another day!). However, rather than write it off, I saw this as an opportunity to gather data, to observe and understand a different lifestyle, to see a different part of the world, and to evaluate if this was something I'd be interested in pursuing.

Truly being in the moment recognizes that there will be time to reflect...later. There's time to embrace the moment, to soak in all of the sensations without being concerned with the end result. You get to immerse yourself in a moment, a culture, a city, a conversation, an experience for that precise time; don't miss it by rushing to a result or a destination.

Step 2: Observe

"Who is this second party that is aware that you are aware? The answer is your true self. The one who is talking is your ego or personality. The one who is quietly aware is who you really are, the Observer. The more you become aligned to the quiet Observer, your true self, the less you judge."
—THOMAS STERNER, *The Practicing Mind*

Part of being present in these experiences is examining how we feel, what we see, and how the experience itself is impacting us in the moment. We should take it all in! It's also important to note that negative experiences are just as beneficial as positive ones. In fact, I think we have the opportunity to learn *even more* from our negative experiences. So don't shut your observation skills down when you're in the midst of a miserable experience. Remember, the goal is to create memory royalties, not simply "positive experiences."

The man I was meeting with in Puerto Rico had communicated a desire to improve infrastructure and opportunities in indigenous areas of Puerto Rico. I was interested to see how this high-profile celebrity engaged with the world, if his actions would align with his lofty goals. My first morning in his home, I stood staring at his very fancy, very un-user-friendly coffee maker, wondering how on earth to interpret all of the buttons. He stopped mid conversation, walked across the room, and made me a cup of joe. This spoke volumes to me. Even though this is a person that moves at a million miles a minute, he is aware of his surroundings, cares about his guests' comfort, and will give of his own time for someone else. He is a servant leader. And I observed: his actions aligned with his words.

Part of observing involves paying close attention to your surroundings. It also means focusing on your breath, something that you can control. This helps put you in the moment, drawing you back to what's happening around you, and allowing you to connect with your senses. It also helps you let go of things you don't have control over. It's easy to get wrapped up in a thought spiral that has nothing to do with your immediate circumstances, but focusing on your breath calms the nerves and the mind and reminds you of what's important in the moment.

When we're able to examine ourselves in the midst of an experience, we can also tap into our power to choose. If we start to notice that we're leaning toward negativity, helplessness, or despair, we can actively choose to think differently in these moments and change our experience *as it's happening*. We can question ourselves before we get carried away by negative emotions.

Step 3: Reflect

"Suffering ceases to be suffering at the moment it finds a meaning."
—VISHEN LAKHIANI, *The Buddha and the Badass*

At some point—in all of our experiences—we have to move out of observation mode and into a time of reflection. This shift varies based on the experience or situation, often beginning when the experience itself is over. But sometimes reflection happens in the midst of the experience itself. It's a deeper process of thought, self-awareness, and application, and it's something we often miss out on. In order to genuinely learn and grow from our experiences, we have to take the time to ask ourselves questions like:

- How was that experience for me?

- What did I learn?

- What would I do differently?

- What would I like to do again?

- When was I happiest?

- When was I most uncomfortable?

- How can I apply this to my own life?

- How does it change the way I think?

I'm what I call a "forced extrovert." I love being around people, but I also *need* time alone, and I reach a point in social situations when I can feel myself growing weary. In these moments, I try to take a break and remove myself (you might consider me a Houdini) in order to rest and refuel. This is part of my reflection process: when I've taken a lot in—conversations, observations, advice, stories, etc.—I need time by myself to integrate all of this information. To ask myself questions, to perceive all that I've learned, and to apply these things to my own journey. This may look different for you, but the reflection process is an important part of growing and expanding.

Reflection also involves gleaning wisdom from negative experiences. If we only have positive encounters, we don't fully appreciate them. But we have a tendency to fall into a victim mindset when we face negative experiences: *Why did this happen to me?* Instead, if we take the time to reflect deeply on these encounters—being open to growth and revelation—we can reframe these times as learning opportunities and walk away from them with valuable insights that can inform our future decisions and outcomes. If we can let go of our attachment to things turning out the way we want them to, we will have so many more opportunities to learn, where even our negative experiences can have a positive spin, ultimately making our lives more fulfilling and enjoyable. It also makes us more grateful for the good times, opening our eyes to the abundance that surrounds us when things *are* going our way.

In Puerto Rico, I spent several hours with the celebrity we went to meet with—five of us brainstorming and bouncing ideas off each other about his business. It was incredible: a bit chaotic and fast-paced, but absolutely inspiring. I was in the moment: listening, engaging, asking questions, and soaking it all up. I learned a ton, but I had to take time after that lunch to process and solidify my own take-aways. What I concluded was this man is motivated by doing things other people aren't willing to do. He authentically wants to be a part of change and is willing to be on the ground level, to get his hands dirty getting things started, when many people would shy away.

Witnessing his passion firsthand impacted me. Like all great leaders, he's had missteps along the way, but he has kept going. He has looked for other solutions and not given up. And I saw myself in him, as a person who also finds joy in building and developing. After reflecting on our conversation, I was inspired to keep going, to continue trying to make a change, and to hopefully inspire others to live with more purpose.

But I wouldn't have been able to put words to it had I not paused to reflect:

- What did I learn?

- What did I see?

- How does this change my perspective?

And I'm certainly not done reflecting on this experience. It will continue to be a part of my own journey, impacting how I view certain opportunities. This is a loop, a continuous journey. There is no destination! We get to continually reflect upon our experiences and make new decisions about them. If we remain open to growth and change, our perspectives will shift. Therefore, we may find that previously positive experiences take on a different light, maybe even lose their luster, and we get to adjust accordingly.

In order to pivot and make changes, you have to first understand the underlying issue. Imagine walking into a doctor's office with excruciating head pain. After explaining your symptoms to the doctor, she says, "I don't know what's going on with you. Sorry. Keep on keepin' on."

No exams, no blood tests, no team of specialists. Just a depressing non-diagnosis and a pat on the butt.

Now, obviously this wouldn't happen at the doctor's office, but we do this with our experiences all of the time. We ignore our responses, repress emotions, and try to just move on. While there are times in our lives when we simply have to keep moving—like Dory: "just keep swimming"—if we don't take the time to reflect, these emotions and experiences can build up and overwhelm us. And then, sometimes, we are sideswiped by an experience and we can't move on.

It reminds me of throwing my back out. Prior to that shocking moment, I had noticed pain in my body: my knees were hurting, my lower back was aching, and my whole body was stiff when I woke up in the morning. These were all signs that I needed to stretch, perhaps lose weight, take it easier, but I wasn't willing to slow down. So then— bam—I threw my back out and I was *forced* to slow down and take time off. I was physically incapable of pushing through, and my recovery was long and slow. What would have happened if I had addressed the warning signs? If I had taken the time to reflect on how I was feeling and implemented activities (or eliminated activities) that would have encouraged healing in my body? Maybe I wouldn't have thrown my back out.

The same is true of our emotional experiences. We can shove things down, ignore warning signs, and try to just keep swimming. But at some point, these things will catch up to us. And the ensuing emotions—panic, fear, anxiety, grief, depression—may stop us dead in our tracks. Then we have an even longer, more painful journey toward healing. When we choose not to uncover the cause of our own happiness and dissatisfaction, it's similar to a doctor refusing to examine the cause of our pain. There is something beneath the surface that's causing these feelings, and it's our job to dig in, examine, and process these root causes in order to make necessary changes.

Step 4: Implement

"The secret of being wrong isn't to avoid being wrong! The secret is being willing to be wrong. The secret is realizing that wrong isn't fatal."
—SETH GODIN, *Tribes*

The goal of reflection is implementation: to determine how an experience impacted you and ultimately decide what to do with that. You take action and move forward, with new knowledge in hand. Do you want to do it again? Do you want to invest more time into it? Do you need to pivot? Do you need to eliminate it entirely? We reflect in order to live more intentionally, to invest in more memory royalties, to take control of the things we can, and to pursue more purpose and joy into our lives.

For example, my editor just spent a month in Dubai. Her original plan was to head to the Maldives from there. She originally said "hell yes" to a trip to the Maldives, but after spending two weeks in Dubai, changed her mind.

When I asked why, she said, "I was so inspired by Dubai, I wanted to stay longer."

In this example, Lisa pivoted. She changed course, based on her reflections. This is difficult for many people because we often live in an "I deserve" mentality: *I deserve for my experiences to look a certain way. I deserve for things to pan out the way I expect. For my trip to be fun for all. To not get sick. To be good at everything.* Then, we get stuck there, not growing, learning, or changing. Part of implementation is embracing when things don't go our way and not becoming paralyzed by the unexpected. Sometimes this means changing plans in the middle of a vacation. Other times, it means making a decision to not do something again. Sometimes it's as simple as being grateful.

Gratitude is a wonderful example of implementation. It flies in the face of a victim mentality and entitlement. It's embracing a perspective—regardless of the outcome, good or bad—of "I can find something to be thankful for": an amazing time with family, a lesson learned, an incredible meal, a kind stranger.

My time in Puerto Rico has been added to my memory royalty portfolio. The time I spent with my client was invaluable—we shared meals, laughs, and enlightening conversations. We are closer than ever because of that trip, and now I know more about him, his family, his goals, and what he's looking for when (and if) he does decide to sell his business. (I also learned I won't return to Puerto Rico during the chaos of spring break!) I am thankful for the time I got to spend there, with interesting people, in a new place I really enjoyed.

When we take our reflections and turn them into thankfulness, we solidify our growth, our expectation for more, and infuse our lives with positivity.

Step 5: Move On

"The wound is the place where the Light enters you."
—RUMI

As my kids got older, I learned quickly that our vacations involving early morning excursions were things of the past. I love the mornings! It's when I feel most alive and alert and attentive. I love getting up and getting out the door, seeing the world when it's fresh and new. My kids, on the other hand, haven't seen the morning light (unless that's when they are crawling into bed!) for several years now.

When I first realized this, I was disappointed. I had planned a vacation with several morning activities, and much to my dismay, I heard an earful every morning: *I don't want to go. Why do we have to get up so early? Dad, this is vacation!!* While it was a bummer to me, I had two choices: keep trying to force it, or move on.

Going against my dad's best advice of "buck up and carry on," I actually decided I needed to move on. I wasn't going to change my kids' ways with a dissertation on the joys of the morning. It quite frankly wasn't worth the relational turmoil and emotional exhaustion. My goal is not to control my kids and make decisions for them. In the vacations to come, I simply got up and did my own thing, often by myself, and scheduled our family outings for the afternoon.

We would save ourselves a whole lot of heartache and energy if we adopted this mentality on a daily basis. If we could see the things we don't have control over, let go of unmet expectations and disappointments, and simply move on. We adopt this sense of detachment we talked about and don't let negativity fester and consume us. We take control of what we can—our own mindset, our own perspective—and we move forward toward something good and constructive.

Like my grandma said, "Let's take a break." I was clearly getting frustrated with the puzzle and she clearly had an adult perspective of: *It's not worth this level of frustration.*

When we get into these negative mindspaces, it's difficult to see solutions, to think critically, and to detach ourselves from a particular destination (like completing the puzzle). But stepping away, taking a breath, doing something totally different often allows us to re-enter that space with a fresh outlook and resolved energy. It also gives us time to evaluate whether or not that task is worth completing. *Is finishing the puzzle that important to me? Or can I put the puzzle away, be done with it, and feel 100 percent okay with that decision?*

One of our clients once said, "He who forgets the quickest wins." I love this mentality because it circles back to the idea of attachment. If we get too fixated on our failures, on the things that didn't work, we choose to be stuck. We start honing in on the lack in our lives, falling into the trap of that "deserve" mentality. You only get one life and every day you're one step closer to death, so feeling sorry for yourself and focusing on the negative is a waste of precious time. On the other hand, when we're able to move on and detach ourselves from particular outcomes, we remain open to more experiences, recognizing that every single day is new and different and therefore the outcomes can change.

We also have to be willing to reevaluate how we think about things. If, upon reflection, we realize that a thought, a habit, or an experience isn't serving us anymore, isn't bringing joy or life or goodness, then it's okay—in fact, it's vital—to let that thing go and change. Again, the only thing we truly have control over is ourselves and the present moment. We can't change something that's happened to us in the past. But we can (and often do) allow that thing to haunt us, to fester, to continuously create tension and turmoil and frustration. While it's a difficult thing to do, moving on is the only way to release the grip this particular thing has over us and not allow it to define or impact our days moving forward.

Step 6: Find the Silver Lining

"Eat a live frog first thing in the morning and nothing worse will happen to you the rest of the day."
—MARK TWAIN

This quote helps me remember to cultivate gratitude in my life.

Even in the most difficult situations, you can find something good, something worth taking away. These findings should be incorporated into the Feedback Loop, too. Having gratitude for what you *do* have helps shift your focus from what's lacking. You're more proactive because you feel less threatened, less worried about what's lurking around the corner. This allows you space to operate at a higher consciousness, to be more creative, and to see more possibilities.

Finding the silver lining is a choice. Choosing positivity is a choice. The reality is, if you *choose* negativity, no amount of coffee or good news or nice people can help you find the good. The great news is that we have control over our outlook. We can choose how we see our circumstances and how much we learn from our experiences and what we'll implement or walk away from. These are all choices.

If I had gone to Puerto Rico hoping that this celebrity would become one of our clients or one of my new best friends, I would have walked away incredibly disappointed. In reflecting on the trip, I could focus on the negative: the spring break vibe was out of control; I only got three hours with this guy. Or I have the choice to see the good: I spent quality time with a client and friend; I got to meet amazing people; I can't wait to bring my kids to Puerto Rico someday. And I got to go to Puerto Rico, a beautiful, lively, intriguing country that I hadn't been to before. What a gift! We get to frame and interpret our experiences with silver lining—we are in control of this.

Truth: if you eat a live frog first thing in the morning, it gives you perspective for the rest of your day. There are very few things that I can imagine that would be worse than taking a bite of a warm, squirmy, squishy frog…and then proceeding to chew it up and swallow it. You get the picture. This is an absolutely disgusting way of saying that you have to continuously put your circumstances into perspective. There's almost always something worse. This process helps you see the good, recognize what you do have control over, and embrace the glitches with more flexibility, humor, and grace.

Implementing the Loop

"Principles: Life and Work, in which I struggle with conflicts, reflect on them, write down the principles I derive from them, and then improve them—and do that over and over again, in a never-ending, evolutionary way that I describe as 'looping.'"
—RAY DALIO, *Principles for Dealing with Change*

As we choose to show up, evaluate, reflect, and implement— as we get better at the Feedback Loop—all of the moments become opportunities to inform our future decisions.

Do I take a break like Grandma would suggest? Or do I embody Dad and act like a duck? (Please note that I have learned so much more from both my grandmother and my dad, but that is a book for another day!)

Because we're able to pursue things that we know are life-giving and joyful, we will start to live a more intentional, well-rounded, fulfilling life. We will get better at avoiding experiences that aren't enjoyable (if we can), and we will start to see the less-than-perfect experiences as learning and growth opportunities. Nothing is wasted.

And, inevitably, this more intentional way of living will lead to more purpose and more fulfillment. It's impossible to live in a victim mindset when you start to take ownership over your experiences, when you start to reframe negative experiences as learning opportunities, when you start to build a portfolio of memory royalties that enhance your life, and when you start to see the silver lining in even the worst of experiences. These things aren't happening *to* you, they are happening *for* you. They are all tools on your journey. And these are the moments that make life worth living, that define your unique race that is worth running, because it's yours.

CHAPTER 10

The Value of Your Journey

"If you ain't first, you're last."
—RICKY BOBBY, *Talladega Nights*

I REMEMBER HEARING A STORY ABOUT AN OLYMPIC archery competitor (who knows—maybe someone made it up, or perhaps I dreamt it!). She didn't win a medal, but spent years training for the Olympics. She would wake up before her kids every day and train for hours.

In the interview, she was asked, "You sacrificed all of this time and you didn't get the gold. How does this make you feel?"

Her response was: "I didn't sacrifice anything. This is how I chose to live. This is what I *wanted* to do. I made *choices*, not sacrifices."

The interviewers were trying to get at something: that this woman had wasted time because she didn't have a gold medal to show for it. But her response was so beautiful and enlightening because it pointed at gratitude and the value of her journey, not an accomplishment. She didn't see her choice as a sacrifice or a waste because she was able to do what she loved every day. She got to practice and compete in an activity that brought her joy and life. She got to experience the journey and prove to herself that she could get there. The gold medal wasn't her only motivation—the overall *experience* was, too.

Lifestyle Management

Memory royalties help you experience all life has to offer and live a life that's uniquely yours; memory royalties help you run your own race.

Sometimes, when our clients leave our office, I'll say something like: "May you experience all life has to offer you." It probably catches people off guard—not something you'd expect your wealth manager to throw at you!—but I want to brighten up people's days. There's no shortage of things to worry about, and I like to think that sending our clients on their way with a positive blessing of sorts might just change their "business-as-normal" mentality.

Cheesy as it sounds, it encompasses what our organization desires for each of our clients—to realize there is so much good to experience in life, but we have to be willing to look for it until we find it. We don't believe in just crunching numbers (though we do it and we are very good at it). We, first and foremost, want to know our clients and talk to them about their goals, dreams, and ambitions. We want to discuss how we can help them to run their race!

At Clarity, we strongly believe in this idea of lifestyle management. It's not just about your financial portfolio. How and where you invest your money is a reflection of your lifestyle. Your memory royalties are too.

Remember Deborah? Her *new* memory royalties are a reflection of her *new* lifestyle. She is currently renting a place in Texas to help her decide whether she wants to move there permanently. The memory royalties she's creating demonstrate that she is adventurous, willing to try new things, and ready to live her life to the fullest.

It's a balancing act: the team at Clarity and I want to take great care of your wealth and encourage you to live a meaningful life. We recognize that every person is different, there is no perfect "allocation plan," there are countless choices, and there will be bumps and wiggles along the way, no matter the course.

While we don't tell our clients how to live, we do offer advice based on our experiences and knowledge. We've worked with hundreds of clients and families and therefore have a wealth of experience to draw upon to help make sure others don't make the same mistakes twice (i.e., only pay tuition once!). We help our clients evaluate decisions by offering pros and cons, and we draw upon successes and learning experiences to inform and shape future decisions.

For example, one of our families bought a home in Kauai when their children were young, and they spent Thanksgiving to Christmas there every year for over a decade. But now, their kids are grown, they have families of their own and demanding jobs, and no one has been over there in a few years. They are starting to feel like this asset has become a "liability":

- Do they rent it out?

- Sell it?

- Save it for their children or grandchildren?

This isn't the first time we've faced this particular conundrum. Several of our clients have invested in partnerships on boats, sharing the cost with a couple of friends and dividing up usage time. In the beginning, it sounded like a great idea to them, but inevitably it turned into a liability. (As they say, "The two best days in a boat owner's life are the day they buy a boat and the day they sell it.") They couldn't use it when they wanted to. The boat broke down during their week on the water (and who has to pay to fix it?). They had to pay to dock it, to store it, to winterize it, etc. They moved further away from the water and it wasn't as appealing. The same thing has happened with planes (I have my own experience with this!). There are unexpected costs and unexpected complications with owning an asset like this that aren't apparent prior to actually experiencing it. This is the beauty of learning from other people's mistakes—you don't actually have to live them! You can weigh the pros and cons from an informed vantage point and therefore make a fully informed decision.

Many of our families have assets that lose their luster for different reasons, and we've had the opportunity to walk with clients through this difficult process several times. Which means, we not only have a financial perspective to offer, we also have real-life options that have worked (and not worked!) for other people. The ultimate goal is to help expedite each client toward experiencing their best life as the seasons change and priorities shift.

What You Can't Control

Some people prioritize being the best.

Let me tell you something: there will almost always be someone better than you. Better looking. Better skilled. Better positioned. Better at cooking. Better at math. You name it—someday, someone will surpass you in your specific skill set. In the race of life, there isn't a first place. You've either lived *your* best life or you haven't. This isn't meant to be disheartening. On the contrary, this is meant to free you up, so you quit trying so hard to be the best and embrace all of your unique desires and attempts. Because *you don't have* to be the best. And the silver lining? While you can't control who is better than you, you *can* control what you can learn from them.

You have no control over the market or the ultimate value of your assets. You do, however, have control over how much these uncontrollables consume you. And if you were to invest more time into memory royalties, it would draw your attention away from obsessing over market fluctuations and toward curating memory royalties.

While we make the best of plans, we have to face the fact that something will likely go not-as-planned (insert "'wrong"). In fact, we should *expect* it. And while the temptation is to crawl in a hole, resort to a "deserve" mentality, or to war against this outcome, remember these are the moments that have the most to teach us: failure is the best instructor.

When life takes a sharp turn, it's important to pause and enter into the journey with even more attention and care.

- What can you learn here?

- What can you see?

- How will this change your perspective, your insight, your strategy moving forward?

- Who are you becoming on this path?

This last question is worth taking a pause for. This is an important part of your process: who are you becoming? How are you growing and changing? How are the decisions you are making in the moment affecting the future version of yourself? If you have personal goals in mind—characteristics you want to embody, ways you want to evolve, perspectives you want to adopt—you can then evaluate your decision-making and responses to circumstances with this goal in mind.

This requires a depth of self-awareness that takes time to cultivate. We are all becoming someone—parents, grandparents, business owners, and world adventurers. It's a beautiful thing to continue evolving, to recognize that you're not done, and embrace a life of continuous growth and transformation.

WE WILL SEE

There's a parable about a Zen master in a village.

In this parable, people visit this Zen master every day with varying ailments, seeking his advice and wisdom.

One day, he was approached by a man who was filled with sorrow that his son had lost the use of his legs and was unable to run with the other boys.

The Zen master said to the man, "We will see."

Months later, when many of those young boys were drafted into the military, this man's son was spared because of his disabled legs.

The moral of the story? We don't know what the future holds. This parable points to the simple truth that we don't quite know how something that might seem "bad" or like we're "missing out" might lead to some other blessing. For example, there are stories of people who unfortunately missed their flights on 9/11 or were too sick to arrive for work at the Twin Towers. Their in-the-moment inconveniences likely saved their lives.

If we could accurately predict the future, how boring might life be? The surprises, the bad and good ones, give color to our lives, provide necessary contrast, and help us uncover all that life has for us to receive and share.

Imagine approaching this same Zen master, troubled about what to do with your money. You tell him you have a certain amount in the bank, but you're concerned about inflation, deflation, or all of your money disappearing.

And his response is, "We will see."

We don't know what the future holds, and there is so much we *don't* have control over. But when we accept the idea that money is tokenized time, we can use a portion of our wealth to take hold of *some* of the life we want *right now* and choose not to live in fear of the future. We can embrace the unknowns, trusting that even when things seem "bad," there is likely hidden goodness in the struggle. And we can keep on living in the moment, investing our tokenized time into more experiences that can shape us and impact our loved ones.

ALTER YOUR PATH

"The Plan" implies an immovable, unmalleable path, one way to go. "Stick to the plan," we say, as if there's a formula, a step-by-step process that will unquestionably lead to said destination or the peak of success. When we talk about *one* plan, we don't leave room for diversions, for life's inevitable curve balls, or even for personal growth and change in a different direction. We get too attached to *one* outcome, when life simply doesn't work this way.

Planning, on the other hand, is a valuable process. We spend time considering various options, trying to stay unattached to a specific outcome, with an open mind and a realization that we'll be doing more planning down the road. Planning (as in an action and an ongoing process) leaves room for flexibility and course shifts and life's surprises! It helps us find joy in the unexpected, learning opportunities in our "failures," and acceptance in the midst of new experiences.

As I've said before, our ability to adapt is one of our superpowers. That means a deep commitment to plan*ning* (as in, an ongoing action), rather than a deep commitment to a plan (as in, a set course). If we commit to plan*ning*, we leave room for an ongoing process and create space to reevaluate and shift directions, if needed. If we commit to getting good at planning as an ongoing process, we open ourselves up to the possibility of finding more possibilities, taking the path less traveled, or blazing an entirely new trail.

Live a Memorable Life

"Planning is everything, the plan is nothing."
—PRESIDENT DWIGHT EISENHOWER

Unlike the story of the Olympic archer, many people focus solely on the win. Whether that's a certain number in their bank account, a job title, or their kid getting into a specific school, they get wrapped up in idolized destinations and forget to see the goodness along the way. They fall into the trap of believing they have to be the best at something in order to enjoy it, and then they forget to celebrate the everyday victories and acknowledge the joy of simply getting to *do* something or *be* somewhere—they forget the importance of memory royalties.

I will never forget, during my days as a portfolio manager, meeting with a client as he was dying of kidney failure in a hospital bed. As the oldest of three siblings, he had taken over his family's auto business and had accumulated great wealth. But along the way, he had lost touch with his siblings, burned bridges, and was all alone. That day, he looked me in the eyes and said, "I'll give you a billion dollars if you can find someone to give me a kidney."

I was at a loss for words. Here was a man who had "arrived" by some standards—a person who had produced and earned and accumulated and had the bank account and the assets to prove it. And yet...

"I worked so hard to be the best at this," he said, "And I forgot to smell the roses along the way." This man was willing to give up all of his wealth for just a little more time. And while that's maybe an extreme case, too many of us relate, as we focus the majority of our time and energy on wealth accumulation at the expense of true happiness and real relationships.

This realization—that so many people sacrifice joy and fun and connection for the sake of accumulating wealth—has transformed our approach to wealth management at Clarity. Don't get me wrong, we have clients and team members that take memory royalties very seriously, people who look for opportunities to connect with their spouses, their children, friends, and each other. While our clients request financial insights (and we provide 'em), we also want them to embrace the idea of creating memory royalties. There's more to learn, new opportunities to explore, and creative experiences they haven't been exposed to before!

As we partner with our clients, we are so blessed and grateful to learn *with* them as they share their memory royalties with us. Just the other day, a couple I've worked closely with for many years was preparing for a vacation abroad, the first trip without their son, now a teenager. Over my time working with this family, their wealth has grown from $400K to tens of millions of dollars, and I've seen them make incredibly wise and thoughtful decisions throughout the years.

Before they left on their trip, they told their son to call me first if anything happened to them. That I would help guide him. I was honored by this—it is exactly why I do what I do. I value my relationships with our clients, serving them, gaining their trust, and helping them create lives they love and leave lasting legacies for generations to come.

What is the point of accumulating wealth if you can't look back and say you lived a memorable life?

I want everyone in my life—my family, friends, and clients—to experience all it has to offer; I want them all to have a treasure chest full of memory royalties so they can run their own race and live a life of fulfillment.

I want this for you too. So, what are you waiting for? Grab a pen and piece of paper, jot down a few ideas (or ten!) and start to curate memory royalties. Your life is yours to live, so live it!

Conclusion

"The best-laid plans of mice and men go oft awry."
—ROBERT BURNS

WHEN CARLA BEGAN EVALUATING HER WEALTH FROM a broader perspective—as an opportunity to craft a life that she could love—she was able to release bitterness, resentment, and fear. She saw a bright future, full of abundance and freedom to pour into herself and her loved ones. She transformed, inwardly and outwardly. Happiness can do this.

But this transformation didn't happen overnight. Carla had deep attachments—to her husband's view of money, to the media's portrayal of the economy, to her own beliefs that life should have turned out differently for her. She had to actively release these agreements over and over again, detach herself from negativity, and identify the things that *do* bring her joy and meaning, things that were worth investing in.

Invest in Meaningful Experiences

I ask you this: at the end of your days, do you want to be sitting on a pile of money? Or do you want to be remembering all of the wild, fun, beautiful things you did with the people you love?

I began writing this book with the hope of helping people. After thirty years of conversations and interactions that left me wondering: *why are so many wealthy people unhappy?* I knew that something needed to change. No amount of money can guarantee happiness. So I asked myself the question: *What does? And what opportunities does money afford that can help me and our clients experience more meaning and more joy?*

It didn't take long to realize that our view of wealth management was the first thing that had to change. If we were only focused on accumulation—as the accumulators and as wealth managers—we were missing something. There's more to wealth than just...well, *more*. This accumulation is actually the opportunity, if we start to see it as tokenized time, as a conduit to create lifelong memories that enhance our lives.

Memory royalties create value and meaning in life like nothing else can. But it's not just about checking a to-do off a list: "We went on our yearly family vacation to Florida, CHECK." Memory royalties are more about adopting a mentality of investing into meaningful experiences. Anything—a walk, a dinner date, a trip, a dance lesson, a new degree—that adds value and variety to your days and months and years. Memory royalties allow you to look at life from a different vantage point:

- What do you care about?

- What are your goals and dreams?

- Who do you want to spend time with?

Whether good or bad, memory royalties hold lessons for each one of us. They stretch us and awaken us; they help us stay curious and hopeful; they make us feel something and require our presence and awareness.

Choose to Fully Engage

"Doubt is not a pleasant condition, but certainty is an absurd one."
—VOLTAIRE

We can't just show up and hope for the best. No, life requires a bit more involvement on our part. And this is where the magic happens. When we choose to fully engage: to block off time for the things that matter, to intentionally diversify our experiences, to think critically about our time and wealth, and to let our experiences shape us and transform us into better versions of ourselves. This is when we start to tap into more value, more happiness, more meaning.

Only then are we able to experience the fullness of life, the richness of relationships, and the beauty of these memory royalties that don't tarnish or degrade over time. We can't take any of these things with us when we die—not our money or our "things" or even our loved ones. But we can be proud of the life we lived, proud of the choices we made, and proud of the people we loved. This looks different for every single person—truly, only you know what will make you proud. Only you know what will make you happy. It's not a formula or a one-size-fits-all. It's a journey. And it's *your* journey, so run your own race!

And perhaps that's one of the biggest lessons I've learned in this process of evaluation, reflection, and detachment— that the journey is, in fact, *the destination*. Instead of defining our lives by invisible milestones, marked by a number in the bank or a title plaque on a desk, maybe we could define our lives by the everyday journey. The joy, belief, kindness, and goodness we infuse into the people around us, into ourselves.

I truly believe that this is part of our role as wealth managers, to walk alongside our clients as they seek to find meaning in their lives, as a guide and a friend. We can offer ideas on how to diversify, not just their financial portfolio, but their life portfolio. Especially because we have a broad perspective, having worked with a variety of clients and families, and we can pull from this wealth of knowledge and wisdom to help others along the way. There's no sense in making the same mistake twice, and we can learn not only from ourselves but also from those who have gone before us.

There is more to life than wealth accumulation. Maybe you know that. Maybe you simply hope that's true. Maybe you think I'm full of it (but I am not attached to any outcome!). Regardless, I encourage you to ask yourself one question. Or take this question to your inner circle: What's something you haven't done before that you really want to do? Start there. Do it. And see how this one thing starts to shift the landscape of your life.

Acknowledgments

"What is it you plan to do with your one
wild and precious life?"
—MARY OLIVER

ALL ALONG THIS BOOK JOURNEY, I HAVE BEEN ASKED why I am writing it. My answers have ranged from "To see if I can" to "I want my children (now young adults) to know more of what I'm about, why I do what I do." (It is also a mea culpa for all my time spent away from them.)

Perhaps I also want to test my perspective. Life is shaped and reshaped often as events transpire, both better and worse than others (as opposed to simply "good" or "bad" circumstances)…

Perhaps I desire to show that behind some stoic outer layer, we are all still more like each other than we are different.

Perhaps I also want to help mitigate the polarizing angst in the media and market—to help (in at least some small way) everyone have the opportunity to do and be the best versions of themselves.

I am blessed to have all the people in my life, from my loving parents and grandparents, to friends and family (my own and future growing family), business partners, Clarity team members, and our clients and families. I am also blessed with the work hard/ play hard members of Gen Next (now Alder) forum and the business forum, Turning Point, that I have the privilege of spending time with.

In all sincerity, I truly feel very blessed and am overwhelmed with gratitude for absolutely everyone and everything.

About the Author

Todd Rustman is a CFA® (Chartered Financial Analyst), CFP® (Certified Financial Planner), CLU® (Chartered Life Underwriter), and EA (Enrolled Agent). He believes wholeheartedly in Jackie Robinson's famous words: "Life is not a spectator sport."

His success comes from combining quantitative data and analytics with strong Midwest roots, simplifying complex and confusing financial constructs for his clients and families—and reverse engineering their unique needs for personal happiness and fulfillment. When he isn't inspiring others—or, even better, being inspired by them—he enjoys spending time with his wife, Sherry, and children, Sierra and Cayden, in the family's home in Nellie Gail Ranch.